What people are saying about …

NO ELEVATOR TO EVEREST

"Will Acuff is a deep-water soul, a wisdom well, who draws daily from the riches of Christ to pour out life-giving water to all his neighbors and friends. His faith is embodied, and he has walked through great trials and accomplished many a great thing with a humble and authentic joy that is contagious and with a peace that is steady. His lived-out faith has been a deep source of encouragement to me and to our entire city. His delight is to see *all* people flourish, and that is a delight so close to the heart of Christ."

Ellie Holcomb, musician

"My brother has that kind of faith that stays joyful even in the midst of pain. He doesn't run from or ignore the hardship but rather steps into the experience fully, deepening his trust in the Lord every step of the way. In this book, Will takes what he has learned, blends it with contemplative Christianity, and makes it practical. He demonstrates his own process of daily joy and invites us into it for ourselves. This is not a book of theory, but of hard-won wisdom."

Jon Acuff, author, speaker, brother

"God has blessed Will with the unique ability to teach others both the practical and profound when it comes to connecting with the Holy Spirit. Will's thoughtful frameworks and spiritual exercises bring to life a model of engaging with the Spirit that is deeply rooted in God's Word. You couldn't find someone more humbly yet passionately committed to living in the Spirit, who serves as a real-life testimony of the life and heart change that occurs when we open our hearts to the Spirit."

Greg Baumer, author of *God and Money*, Bible Project board member, Nashville business leader

"Over the past year, my family has grown to know Will and his story, and I have been directly impacted by his insight and wisdom that he lives out in his daily life. He has profound discernment in how to find hope and develop perseverance, and he is a sage guide toward creating healthy rhythms and implementing them in an anxious and overwhelming society. I believe his voice is a steady source of wisdom and encouragement that is desperately needed in our world today."

Hillary Scott, musician, Lady A

"In *No Elevator to Everest*, Will Acuff takes us on a courageous journey through pain and joy, offering a deeply moving testament to God's transformative power. His transparency invites readers to shed superficial faith and embrace a life rich with self-awareness, emotional resilience, and intimate connection with Christ. This book is a gift for anyone seeking to encounter God's tenderness in the midst of life's most challenging seasons. Will's words offer not just hope but a roadmap to soul-deep peace and enduring joy."

Darren Whitehead, senior pastor of Church of the City, Nashville, author of *The Digital Fast*

"Will is a deep and winsome guide on the journey toward a renewed faith in the midst of time and tears. This hard-won, joy-filled guide is a personal but universal invitation to receive a new story, one worth every labored step."

Katherine and Jay Wolf, coauthors
of *Hope Heals* and *Suffer Strong*

"Will Acuff's *No Elevator to Everest* is a powerful invitation to face life's toughest climbs with courage and faith. With grace and humility, Will shares his experiences and practical wisdom, guiding readers through emotional valleys and spiritual growth. This isn't just a book to read; it's a companion for anyone seeking to live with intentionality and resilience, showing that each step brings you closer to God's purpose for your life."

Gabe Turner, senior pastor of The Point

NO ELEVATOR TO EVEREST

Shift from Survive to Thrive through
Spirit-Led Self-Awareness

WILL ACUFF

DAVID **C** COOK

transforming lives together

NO ELEVATOR TO EVEREST
Published by David C Cook
4050 Lee Vance Drive
Colorado Springs, CO 80918 U.S.A.

Integrity Music Limited, a Division of David C Cook
Brighton, East Sussex BN1 2RE, England

DAVID C COOK®, the graphic circle C logo and related
marks are registered trademarks of David C Cook.

The website addresses recommended throughout this book are offered as a
resource to you. These websites are not intended in any way to be or imply an
endorsement on the part of David C Cook, nor do we vouch for their content.

Library of Congress Control Number 2024946324
ISBN 978-0-8307-8791-3
eISBN 978-0-8307-8792-0

The Team: Michael Covington, Stephanie Bennett, Jeff Gerke, Judy
Gillispie, Leigh Davidson, Susan Murdock, Angela Messenger
Cover Design: Brian Mellema

Printed in the United States of America
First Edition 2025

1 2 3 4 5 6 7 8 9 10

010625

*To my wife, Tiffany, the bravest
person I know. I choose you.*

*Raylan and Penelope, one of my greatest desires
in life is that I get to fully know you and be
fully known by you. You are an incredible
gift. I love you just because you are you.*

Contents

Introduction

A Guide to Daily Life in the Spirit

Where shall I go from your Spirit?

Psalm 139:7

I remember feeling like battery acid. Someone had told me that battery acid was so acidic it could chew through anything it touched. So if I was like that, I didn't want anyone near me. I could already visualize the skin-bubbling moment of human interaction.

I was in the depths of a sorrow that seemed without end, and the shallow small talk surrounding me just made me more furious, lonely, and sad. I wanted to have a Samson moment—I thought that if I could just pull the roof down on myself and everyone around me, maybe the pain would end.

But that was not an option. Because I am a Christian. And Christians don't do things like that. Right?

What had brought me to this place? The immediate context was the major depressive disorder that my wife, Tiffany, was experiencing (of the can't-get-out-of-bed variety) and the intensity of my son's multiple disabilities. Both contributed to a daily rhythm that felt like triage, not life.

Underlying all this was a family-of-origin story that said, "We don't get angry, and we don't get sad, because we are Christians." And underneath *that* was a faith tradition that said, "You are a dunghill covered by the white snow of Christ's crucifixion." In other words, you are fundamentally flawed and unworthy of love.

I felt emotionally, spiritually, and physically trapped. I was starting to come undone.

This book is a story of spiritual awakening that has led to a life of tremendous joy.

I want to make it clear at the outset that none of my context changed. What changed was me. I learned how to live a life daily in the Spirit of Christ through the work of Spirit-led self-awareness.

Theologians have said for a very long time that the journey of faith consists of two parts: knowing God and knowing self better.[1] Augustine said it beautifully:

> Let me, then, confess what I know about myself, and confess too what I do not know, because what I know of myself I know only because you shed light on me, *and what I do not know I shall remain ignorant about until my darkness becomes like bright noon before your face.*[2] (emphasis added)

Spirit-led self-awareness is the practice by which the darkness becomes "like bright noon."

This makes all the sense in the world when we consider that the God of the universe created us in love for a loving relationship with Him. We are image bearers. We uniquely reflect His glory. Therefore, as a creation of the Most High, we are worth knowing. To put it another way, it is a really good thing to know yourself.

Yet, broadly speaking, in our Western Christian culture, we have said, "Knowing God is what matters. Knowing self, past the point of acknowledging yourself as a hopeless sinner, is worthless." This is the equivalent of being told that the path ahead is yours to walk, but first you must tie your right foot behind your back. We need both the knowledge of God and the knowledge of self.

Who is this book for? If you grew up in the church, or had a conversion in college at a campus ministry, or are dutifully going to church right now every weekend but just feeling more and more numb—this book is for you.

If you think of yourself as a Christian and then notice a voice of self-attack that condemns you for not being able to "gain victory over that besetting sin"—this book is for you.

If you have left the church thinking, *These church people say they are all about love, but it feels more like control and demands and less like mercy and grace*—this book is for you.

Finally, if you've ever tasted the ecstatic moment of oneness with the Spirit of God and want more of that in your everyday life—this book is for you.

How will this actually work?

It is a huge promise to say that the following pages will bring you on a journey toward a deeper knowledge of yourself and the Spirit of God ... but it is one I can sincerely make *with* you.

With you means we will go together. Every journey needs a guide. This is not the kind of book you can simply read or quickly Audible and then move on from. This is a book of stories, concepts, and practices. The concepts point toward key underlying truths that spark wonder and awe. Also, the practices in this book require just that—practice. That's why I say the promise I make is made *with* you.

So read the concepts in the book, think about them, savor the ideas, and learn how to work them into your heart. Go slowly. Where you come to a practice, learn the practice. Try it on. See if it fits. Find out what it asks of you. See if it feels joyful or hard, like work or like pleasure. Hold it all loosely. This is not a book of demands but of play.

I do not come to you as a researcher, neuroscientist, or psychologist but as a husband and a dad who was desperate to stop hurting so much. What I write here is not theory but practice.

I am reminded of a story about a hopeful climber who set off to conquer Mt. Everest. When she arrived and learned she had to take a guide, she felt frustrated at first. She wanted to be the hero who did it alone. Stumbling one day while crossing a gap in a glacier, the firm grip of the guide saved her life. The reality of the struggle took her to her utmost limits, and she knew she could not have gone alone.

Yet at the same time, the climb required her best. While she could not do it by herself, she was also astounded at her own strength, courage, and conviction. The ascent invited her to reframe her own sense of self. She was more capable than she ever dreamed.

So, while there is no elevator to Everest, there is a guide.

One last thought before you start your climb.

The following stories don't exist in a vacuum. Between some of our most challenging moments were scenes of laughter and that unique delight available so effortlessly to children. Our son, Raylan, has the uninhibited enthusiasm of someone who has never cared what anyone else thinks. When he is excited about something, it is a full-body reaction: head thrown back in a laugh so contagious that you don't know you've joined in until your chest hurts from laughing so hard. He grabs your arm even if you are right there, seeing the exact same thing, as if he wants to take you even closer. There is a bit of "Can you believe this is real?" to his excitement. It is wonderful.

When he is around some of his favorite people, he gently asks them, "Are you my best friend?" Anytime we see a group of kids playing any type of sport, even if it's one he doesn't enjoy (e.g., soccer), he will boldly march into the middle of the game and ask if he can play. He is far braver than me on the social front.

One of his favorite pastimes is scaring himself (and hopefully you). His favorite subject of late is megalodons, the ancient giant cousin to the great white shark. When he really gets himself worked up thinking about them, he rounds every corner—on dry land—looking for one. He will jump out at you if you're walking next to him and just yell, "Megalodon!" He smirks with delight thinking that you too are just as terrified of this ancient ocean-dwelling monster. Raylan is an incredible kid.

I would consider it a tragedy if you read this book and came away thinking I don't treasure my family. What follows is real, often raw, and has frequently brought me to the end of myself. But my deep love and affection for my entire family, and the Lord's abiding mercy, held me time and time again. I am also deeply aware that I don't know what it was like to be inside Raylan's mind and body in some of the most difficult moments. As hard as it was for Tiff and me, I imagine it was far more challenging for him. As you read this book, I pray you read it with the backdrop of the desperate tenderness with which it was written.

Chapter 1

The Spirit in You

Our true self is a self in communion.

James Finley, *Merton's Palace of Nowhere*

I'm at a trauma retreat center, and I don't want to be.

It is the end of day one, and the chip on my shoulder communicates, "I am here so that my wife feels better and I learn how to make her better. I have created a fortress of solitude and do not need anything, thank you very much."

Before I head to bed, I go to brush my teeth. At that moment, I realize I didn't bring toothpaste. My roommate's toiletry bag is sitting on the bathroom counter. He doesn't have much toothpaste. It's rolled down to the tip. I am thinking judgy thoughts about why this roommate doesn't have fresh toothpaste. (And no, I don't feel any sense of irony.) I carefully squeeze out just one unnoticeable drop of Crest. Some part of me thinks, *Is this what I've come to: stealing toothpaste at a trauma camp in the middle of nowhere because my family is falling apart and I can't stop it?*

The feeling is sharp and rushes from my stomach to my head. I force it down. I won't look at it. I won't go there. Instead, I go to sleep. Thank God for melatonin gummies.

When Tiffany first suggested I go to this retreat center, my exact response was, "Hasn't our family been therapized enough?" I wasn't opposed to therapy in theory, but the idea of being trapped with strangers for multiple days felt claustrophobic. Some deep part of me realized that if I went there, I couldn't hide. It was too vulnerable. However, Tiffany had been to the center herself just a few months prior, and I had seen sparks of hope in her for the first time in years. Years.

That hope spoke to me. Also, she implied that she was drawing some sort of line in the sand about me going. She is an Enneagram eight,[1] and that personality type could be summarized as *knife fighters who don't back down from a challenge*. I knew she was serious.

On day two of trauma camp, we are instructed to begin creating a timeline of our life. We will be visually sharing these with everyone in our small group. Some of us draw pictures; some of us use words. Mine has both, spread over multiple sheets of construction paper. We tape our timelines to the walls behind us so everyone can see. Our instructions are to put down all the events we think have been significant or somehow shaped our life. We are to go year by year and take our time.

What begins to knock the chip off my shoulder is the response of the group to my timeline. My story. I think all of these events are no big deal; the counselor sees trauma. Lowercase- and uppercase-*T* trauma. Sexual abuse as a kid is a capital *T*. A really awful moment with my dad that created a lot of distance gets a lowercase *t*. The counselor points out to me that our brains don't really know the difference between capital *T* and lowercase *t*. It's just a distinction therapists use.

The woman next to me has tears of compassion in her eyes. The overwhelming feeling from the night before rushes back sharply, again starting in my stomach and moving to my head. For a second, I think I might throw up. But then a dull throbbing kicks in, and I begin to weep. Everything I have stuffed away, pushed away, locked away, and forced away starts to become present. Someone in my small group embraces me, and I allow myself, for the first time in decades, to sob.

I am no longer here for Tiff. Now I am here for me.

This begins the journey of what I've come to call Spirit-led self-awareness. It turns out I didn't know *me*. I didn't know how to ask for, much less actually practice, something like, "Search me, oh Lord, and know me." I'd been taught that to "know me" was not important. But this meant I didn't know how to bring myself—my full self—to the Lord. The Lord was standing at the door knocking, wanting to bring full light and life to all parts of me, but I had deadbolted the door against myself ever going there. Which locked Him out, as well.

What follows are stories about my life and the concepts and daily practices that helped me begin to know myself and to shift those deadbolts. What I found on the other side was more daily joy than I ever thought possible.

It has been said that you can't go anywhere to get what you already have. Which begs the question, What do you have? You have your image-bearing self, and you have the living Spirit of God.

What does it mean to *have* in this sense? It means that in your innermost being, your core, these two things are immovable: you are an image bearer, and the Spirit of the living God dwells within you. Neither of these truths, these *haves*, are ephemeral. They are bedrock.

However, many of us have been taught that we cannot trust ourselves. When we believe that, we never get to know ourselves. In fact, we view most of the thoughts, feelings, and internal monologues that flit across the movie screen of our consciousness with distrust and even disgust. Think about it: If you had a new neighbor move in, and someone told you he was a narcissistic liar who was a master at manipulating others, would you be excited to start a relationship with that guy?

We learn to avoid self, to not know self.

And yet we are promised the living Spirit of God, sent by the Father and the Son, to dwell within us. This sets up a tension. We want to avoid that space, that interior place, which we might call "within us." That is where the self resides, and we can't trust that. Yet it is also where the Spirit resides.

We read in Scripture that we are temples of the living God (1 Cor. 6:19). Recently I stayed at a hotel that had long, stretching hallways branching off the lobby in every direction. Down each hallway were rows of locked doors, one after another. I imagine our inner "temple" this way. The Spirit is in the lobby, but we won't let Him anywhere near the locked doors of our heart. We learn to suppress, repress, and generally avoid anything deeply painful. The irony is that only the living power of the abiding Spirit can bring true light to bear in our darkest places.

The Spirit of the living God who dwells within you is—at every moment—whispering divine love to you. He is inviting you into the communion of the trinitarian dance of the Father, Son, and Spirit.

You already have this treasure; it is yours right now. But you may not be experiencing it yet.

How do you move toward this reality? Commit to the journey of Spirit-led self-awareness. Start learning how to walk the trail inward. Start learning how to sit in that space "within." Give it the focus of your conscious mind. What you find there is an infinite treasure of God's love for you in Christ. It is worth any price.

Along the way inward, you will notice that one of your largest blockers is the voice of your inner critic. We all have one (at least one!) voice that slides into our head to tell us how poorly we performed or how we messed up that relationship or that moment.

But hate cannot drive out hate.[2]

You can't silence your inner critic with another voice of attack that says, essentially, "Inner critic, stop being a critic." You are now critiquing your inner critic. This will not work. It only multiplies the inner voice and its power of negativity. You will feel more drained, not less.

Instead, you must befriend your inner critics. With tenderness and compassion, get to know them. Find out what they are fearful of and why they voice certain things so strongly. Ask what they would have you learn and know. Over time, genuine feelings of empathy for yourself will arise. You will connect with yourself in new ways that feel tender and compassionate. You will start to create the opportunity for your inner voice to take on a new job. Maybe a guide, a coach, a teacher ... but not a critic.

Another common question we have as we start this journey inward is, "How do I actually cast my anxieties on the Lord?" It has been my lived experience that casting my fears is more like playing with a yo-yo than throwing a rock in a pond. A yo-yo is attached to your hand.

By definition, it does not leave. It goes out and comes back. There is always a trace line held fast to your finger. But when you throw a rock in a pond, you can see something you once held in your hand actually sinking beneath the water. You once had it, felt its surface and edges, and now you can't see it or even quite remember what it felt like.

Yo-yo life is so common that we think it is the only life. But "perfect love casts out fear" (1 John 4:18), and the Lord has promised perfect love in abundance. Yo-yo life is not for us.

You know what it feels like to wake up with mild anxiety. To run through a litany of moment-by-moment checklists that seek to assert control on the world around you and banish fear to the back of your mind. Until something happens that reminds you of your lack of control, and then the yo-yo snaps back into your palm, the fear moves to the front of your mind, and once again you feel flooded. Somewhere inside you, you know this kind of rhythm cannot be what God intended for His beloved children. Look at the lilies; look at the sparrows. Do not worry.

The Spirit of the living God is not asking us to get really good at the yo-yo. So how do we actually cast away our fears? It all starts with a simple journey inward.

What follows is the first of several *practices* you will encounter throughout this book. Think of a practice as *committing to an intentional activity you believe will yield spiritual growth in your life over time*. If you told me you were committed to getting more sleep but you continued to stay up late every night, I would not believe you actually had a commitment. You might have the beginnings of a desire, but not a commitment. A commitment is always followed by an action. These practices are daily actions.

That said, we must approach this with a sense both of intentionality *and* of self-compassion. You can only start where you are. The emotional-trailhead practice below* is one I'd recommend you try out in the morning right after you wake up. It turns out that *none* of us wakes up "neutral." We wake up with hopes, fears, desires, worries, and task lists. This practice is a way to sort through those initial feelings and use the largest of them like a trailhead into the forest.

Imagine a hiking trail that leads into the woods. At the start of the path, the spot called the *trailhead*, you see a simple sign announcing the name of the trail and where it leads. As you investigate your morning feelings with patience and curiosity, you will naturally walk further into the "forest."

The example below assumes that your primary morning feeling is fear, which is a very common morning emotion for many of us. But yours might be something else.

Get yourself a cup of coffee and move to a quiet place where you won't be disturbed for ten minutes or so. Take a deep breath, and simply notice what you are feeling.

Practice: The Emotional Trailhead

1. Feel the fear and use it to connect with your heart.
   Why are you afraid? How long has this fear been

---

* The trailhead concept originated in Internal Family Systems therapy. I have modified it here as a morning meditation practice that also acknowledges our Christian belief that we have the abiding Holy Spirit. (See Richard C. Schwartz, *No Bad Parts* [Louisville, CO: Sounds True], 24.)

there? What is it connected to? Does it feel massive and overpowering or small yet persistent? When does it show up? Is it cyclical? Circumstantial? Connected to a person in your life? Get curious.

2. Breathe. Contemplating our fear can tighten us up, increase our heart rate, and kick us into fight, flight, or freeze mode. Slowly count to four as you inhale. Then exhale while slowly counting to four again. Slow four counts in, and slow four counts out. This will change your heart rate and in turn calm you down in a meaningful way (i.e., you will feel it in your body).[3]

3. Keep awareness/honesty. As you come to more awareness, stay honest. Don't minimize or hide. Write down what this awareness is bringing you. Do this in a curious and playful way. Don't worry about managing it or making sense. Just write out three to four sentences.

4. Invite the Spirit. Ask the Spirit to lead you. Imagine the Spirit gently taking your hand and walking with you deeper into His life-giving presence and deeper into the inner sanctum in your heart where He has promised to dwell with you forever.

5. Use physical release. Grab hold of a pebble or some other small, solid object. Imagine it as your fear. Name it out loud, if that helps. Squeeze it as tightly as you can. Feel how it bites into your palm. Be

conscious of the way you have to intentionally tell your fingers to stay tight in order to not drop it. To keep holding it is active. Now, hold it at arm's length and simply drop it. It is not yours. Feel the way your hand opens back up to a natural resting position.

6. Savor the feeling of lightness as the fear leaves. Savor the love of God and the guiding of the Spirit. Notice how your heart feels. Welcome this new awareness and this physical sensation of joy and gratitude in the Lord.

You have been a yo-yo master your whole life. This fear might come back. New fears will find their way to you. But when this happens, simply release them again. Since fears and anxieties are so common, we will spend more time dealing with them in the chapters to come.

Walk through this practice daily. Focus on the "largest" emotion you are feeling that morning and start your hike of curiosity inward. You are cultivating awareness, contemplative prayer, and abiding in the Spirit. Engage in this rhythm with a sense of playfulness ... don't take yourself so seriously. The God of the universe loves you, and you are okay. He has you. Over time, this cultivation of awareness and contemplative prayer will have a tremendous effect on the fears in your life.

———

Chapter 2

To Breathe

For the most part all our trials and disturbances
come from our not understanding ourselves.

Jean de La Bruyère, *Les Caractères*

When I walked through my front door after trauma camp, I felt like I was floating. Things had shifted so much internally that it was as if my contact with the normal, everyday, hardwood floor of my house was not quite substantial enough to register.

I was coming home to Tiff, Raylan, and Penelope. I was coming home to a full life that was moving at full speed. Tiffany was waiting in the living room with her parents. They had kindly stayed with Tiff to help out with the kids. There was no way I could have been gone for a full week otherwise. My newly vulnerable self felt exposed just being in their presence. I needed to say so many things to Tiff, but I had to wait until it was just us.

We got a chance that night, on a date to our favorite hole-in-the-wall in East Nashville: Duke's. It's the kind of place where you can get the most incredible sandwich while listening to some obscure indie record at volume eleven. Which is good, because the tables are so small and close together that if it weren't for the music, you'd be in your neighbors' conversation. We had a lot to talk about. I was glad for the deep-cut Afrofuturist hip-hop soundtrack. We leaned toward each other across the table to talk in a near yell.

I tried to explain to Tiff what had happened to me. That I had come into contact with God's abiding love in a way that felt utterly familiar yet completely new. Like meeting an old friend for the first time. I could see that she was trying to understand but not quite getting there. Since Tiff had been at the same trauma camp a few months before me, she knew what I had gone through. She knew all the big concepts I'd been introduced to and the ways the staff crafted an experience that invited you to go deep, even in the context of a small group of strangers.

One of my favorite concepts had been something called the drama triangle, which is a tool to help you understand codependent patterns in your life. This tool will feature prominently in later parts of this story, but on that first date night, it was a shared reference point for Tiff and me. I asked her if she wanted to start using tools and concepts like that in our relationship. She was excited—eager, even—to have me on the journey with her. There was this dawning sense that our marriage, already near the end of its second decade, could experience new vitality.

Then she asked who I had hung out with while I was there. I told her about my small group and how we would all go for a coffee walk in the early morning before breakfast. I gave her a rundown on who was who, introducing her to my new friends through the lens of my fresh memories. I was so enthusiastic. Puppy dog energy, I kept saying, "You are going to love them too!"

Then I noticed this look that might be described as shutting down. She shifted back in her seat, physical distance equating to emotional distance. I leaned in farther, trying to claw back the space. I was confused. "What's wrong?" I asked.

"Some of your small-group friends are girls," she responded.

"Yeah," I said, confused. "I assumed some of your small group were guys, right?"

"Yeah, but I didn't hang out with them on morning walks!" She folded her arms.

I had crossed a line I didn't know was there. I pressed further, still clinging to the idea that everything would immediately be better for us since we had both gone through this trauma intensive. It was the optimism of the newly converted. Everything seemed solvable, including what I perceived as a minor misunderstanding.

"Oh," I said, "but I didn't go on walks alone with any of them. It was a whole big group thing." To my disappointment, this solved nothing.

"We don't do that, Will. We don't have friends like that. I don't have guy friends. You don't have friends that are girls!" Her voice was getting louder. The Afrofuturist hip-hop didn't seem loud enough anymore. People glanced our way.

I reached out my hand, trying to take hers. She kept her arms crossed and doubled down on the glare.

"Honey," I said, "it was not like that at all. I promise. This place gave me the space to be more present in our marriage, not less." My hand was left alone on the table.

"You do not get it, Will!"

Finally, I said, "I'm so confused about what is happening right now. Can we use the drama triangle to try and figure this out?"

"*F*%$ the drama triangle!*" she yelled just as one song came to a close and the bar dropped into a momentary abyss of silence. I'll never forget the look the bartender gave me from twelve feet away as he wiped down a glass. It was pity mixed with that "You okay?" eyebrow lift.

Our date was over.

It took us hours that night to unpack what had happened. We did this in the safety of our home with no prying eyes. She was afraid of the potential emotional intimacy that can happen at a place where people are being so vulnerable. She wanted us to learn how to give that to each other. I wanted that too. But at first, and in my confusion, I was so slow to understand her hurt. But we stayed with it; we leaned into each other.

We deployed all the new communication practices we had learned at trauma camp. We worked back to a place of stability so we wouldn't go to bed angry. Or maybe worse, more confused. It helped us to know each other better.

I woke up the next morning a touch grateful. But overall, I felt dismayed. I genuinely thought we had gone to the same place and had the same experience. I thought we could start this new path of Spirit-led self-awareness together and go at the same pace. It was a beautiful dream, but one fueled by my own codependency. Tiff was telling me that she needed to go slowly and gently. My codependency was demanding that we go together in lockstep.

Codependency is a fascinating concept. Although it has been kicked around since the 1970s, it really came into its own in the 1986 book *Codependent No More: How to Stop Controlling Others and Start Caring for Yourself* by Melody Beattie. The book was an unrivaled success, with millions of copies sold. If you dig a little, you'll find that codependency is not an actual diagnosis but a generalized theory about how humans engage with each other. For the purpose of this book, I'll use it to mean something like, "I'm only okay if you're okay. If you're not okay, I can't be okay."

That night with Tiff, I thought we were both okay. I'd hoped we could start being okay together with a fresh sense of wholeness and a bunch of new communication tools to practice. Wonderful! But she was not okay. And maybe she wasn't okay with me being okay if it didn't align just right with how she wanted that to look for me. Meanwhile, I didn't fully realize I wanted her to approach this with the same speed and intensity that I was. We had one of our most transparent and vulnerable conversations that night, one which I was blessed to have. But the next morning, I woke up deeply disturbed.

Why?

As a codependent person, it was not all right for me to get better if she wasn't also getting better. Further, this "getting better" had to look so similar that I could recognize it. It had to be at the same pace. Imagine a three-legged race at summer camp. That was how I viewed my marriage. We had to time our movements just right to win this thing. And let's be clear: We are trying to win this thing, right? We are trying to do marriage correctly.

But suddenly, we couldn't time our jumps right. I was disturbed that morning because I knew that a brand-new tension had just been introduced to our relationship. Was it all right for me to heal from emotional trauma differently than my wife? Said another way, can I be okay if she is not okay in the same ways? It was as if we'd both been in a car wreck. One of us injured a leg, but the other lost an arm. Tiff's trauma was like losing a limb. The recovery was more significant than my relatively simple leg injury.

The mistimed jumps made me uneasy and afraid. And fear was an old friend.

Perfect Love Casts Out (Some) Fear

I learned 1 John 4:18 as a kid. To me, it meant two things. Number one: God's perfect love, given to you through Jesus, casts out the fear that you will one day go to hell. This made sense to me. I didn't want that kind of existential dread hanging over my young life. Okay, got it. Number two: This perfect love can make you brave.

Bravery was a high value in my family. We were a group of heroes. My grandfather was a war hero who had been a tank commander in WWII and had then fought in the Korean War. My uncle Steve flew jets for the Air Force and was universally regarded as a man not to be messed with. And my dad was a spiritual hero, a warrior for Jesus. A church planter in New England in the 1980s.

At the time, all of our Southern family talked to us as if we were the most sacrificial Christians they knew. We were a pastor's family from North Carolina living in New England, which automatically made us missionaries in their minds, because everyone down South knew the North was utterly lost. They didn't even have sweet tea.

I remember as a kid my dad teaching me all the stories of Samson, David, and (later my favorite) David's mighty men. I could imagine myself with a spear and a shield sneaking through caves, dodging Saul's minions while my heart beat with the unshadowed purity of the righteous. This is who we were as a family.

In my childhood mind, this perfect love of God removed existential dread and gave me a sense of my own hero identity.

What it did not do, and what no one else did, was teach me how to live without all the other fears. I grew up with fears and anxieties in my heart every day, and I didn't know what to do with that. When I looked around, it seemed like everyone else was dealing with fear too. So I thought, *Maybe this is just the Christian life. Maybe we are brave on the big stuff but full of fear on the daily stuff.*

This is actually almost manageable ... if your life stays manageable. As it turns out, however, all of us will hit patches of "unmanageable." Maybe it will be a blip. Just some simple turbulence that gets your attention for a minute but soon lets you get back to your in-flight magazine. For many of us, though, life slides toward a point where we can no longer pretend. The level of pain, suffering, interpersonal friction, and loss gets so profound that the low-grade anxieties snowball into something we must deal with.

My son's journey, along with Tiffany's Complex PTSD* and clinical depression, put me in a place where it was impossible to ignore the daily fears. This hit home one morning when I bit into some oatmeal and a molar crumbled. Have you ever had that tooth dream? You know, the one where a tooth falls out and it is so real and horrible that you wake up and instantly check to see if it really happened? Well,

---

* Complex PTSD is a relatively new diagnosis not yet listed in the current *DSM*. You can read more about it here: www.ncbi.nlm.nih.gov/pmc/articles/PMC5862650.

I lived the tooth dream IRL. Over a bowl of oatmeal, arguably the softest thing I could have been eating that morning.

The dentist explained to me that sometimes, in high stress, we begin to grind and clench our jaws at night. Almost acting as if we were trying to crack walnuts. But it's all subconscious and in our sleep. I had cracked my molar in my sleep without being aware of it. Then, the act of simply chewing on some al-dente oatmeal finished the job. I spit that tooth out in pieces.

The dentist looked at me seriously. "Are you experiencing high stress?"

I nodded with a mouth full of gauze.

"Can you stop the stressful situation?"

I laughed and cried just a little and shook my head no.

He patted my shoulder good-naturedly. "You really should try to lower the stress, Will."

The low-volume fears in my life were now booming, teeth-rattling fears. I had to learn a better way. My body thrummed with the intensity of the anxiety, stress, and pressure. I did not want to lose another molar.

My driving question became, "Does God speak to this kind of fear? The everyday fear that can become crippling fear? The anxieties that can drive us to numb out with the usual: booze, sex, Netflix-bingeing, nonstop-comfort-food eating, work addiction, etc.?" Most of us would say, "Yes, of course He can deal with this kind of fear." But when pressed with the question of *how*, we get quiet.

I have been in countless small groups where someone has brought up something deeply painful, the words dripping with fear, and all of us in the group said things like, "I am so sorry ... that sounds so hard."

And that was it. We prayed for the person, of course. Prayer is real and powerful; I do not want to minimize that in the least. But we didn't know what to do with their pain and fear. We had nothing to give them.

How can the people of God, the people who are in union with the triune Maker of the universe, not have knowledge of the inner workings of our fears and anxieties? Said another way, how can the people who know the Maker not know enough about our internal mechanisms to offer hope and strategies? How can we not move the needle with each other and with ourselves?

How can we keep going around every day with so much fear and just accept it as part of doing life in a fallen world?

Before you get upset, let me say that I'm not suggesting you can override your amygdala, the part of your brain that is credited with controlling the flight, fight, or freeze response. This is an autonomic part of you that God gave you to get out of danger fast. What I am suggesting is that through the journey of Spirit-led self-awareness, you can get to know your fears. You can learn their shapes and rhythms. You can learn the stories that your fears are believing. You can start to unburden those fears, release those fears, and live out of new and better stories. Truer stories.

Fear is not something to ignore, push away, or suppress. Fear actually has the ability to be one of our greatest guides. Fear can show us things that require our conscious attention. Our attention has been likened to a spotlight—when we focus our attention, we can bring illumination to something. When I give my fear gentle attention, I have an opportunity to learn about myself.

Gentle attention is really important. I can notice my fear and come to it with anger: "Ugh, here we go again. I hate this!" But then what I'm really doing is shaming myself. If I come to it with a sense of speed—"Let's get this over with as quickly as possible"—I am dismissing the fear as not that important. But if I approach my fear with a gentleness and a curiosity, I unlock the chance to really, deeply learn from it.

We can liken this to the beautiful truth about Jesus: "A bruised reed he will not break, and a faintly burning wick he will not quench" (Isa. 42:3a). It takes such a gentle hand not to break a bruised reed. It takes slow, steady movements not to extinguish that smoldering wick. To move too fast would be to see the flame go out.

The great thing for the Christian in the journey of self-awareness is that this work is Spirit-led. We never go alone. We have the abiding Holy Spirit, the indwelling presence of the Most High God. So, on those days when the fear feels so big that we can't even get out of bed, let alone do some self-awareness work to really get to know our fear, we can cling to the promise of Jesus. He did not leave us or forsake us. He sent the Helper.

My brother or sister, if you are so paralyzed by fear right now that it seems impossible to ever take one more step, I pray for you to know that you do not take that step alone. I pray you feel the power and the peace of the presence of the Most High within you even now. I pray that you feel His embrace and hear His voice whispering divine love over your life. Even now. Even still. He has you.

I'm just going to assume you'd like to join me in a commitment to no longer sit in fear. In that case, we have to start the process where the theoretical becomes the practical.

For just a second, let's turn to one of the Bible's greatest hits when it comes to fear: "Cast all your anxiety on him because he cares for you" (1 Pet. 5:7 NIV). Awesome. I intellectually believe that. But *how*? How do I cast my anxieties on the Lord? What is the mechanism? That's what we'll talk about soon.

For now, just know that if we are committed to no longer stuffing, repressing, or minimizing our fears, we are on the path to dealing with them.

I remember sitting down with a cup of coffee a few mornings after the fight with Tiff, one molar short, and saying to myself, *I don't know where to start, but I am going to start.*

Start what, exactly? Start to become more self-aware.

If we were sitting down with each other and you asked me how I was feeling about something, and if I were being honest with you, I'd likely start by saying, "I am sad about ..." or "I am afraid of ..." or "I am excited about ..." The particular emotion I might name would change, but do you notice the pattern that emerges at the beginning of each sentence?

I am.

Now, this is not that amazing biblical truth that God is the great I AM—which is one of the most baller statements ever spoken by someone when asked for their identification. This is the lesser "I am." It's the "I am" we use to describe how we are feeling. Notice that we are actually saying, I am my sadness, I am my anger, I am my fear, I am my hurt, I am my happiness, I am my excitement, etc.

These are not mere words. What these "I am" statements point to is our identification with our feelings. We are blended or enmeshed with them, to use psychological terms. We are caught up in them in such a way that we fully associate our state of being with these feelings. When this happens, it is as if we are being taken away by the feelings or that we are somehow victims of our feelings.

We will learn additional emotional skills in the chapters to come, but right now I want us to focus on developing a key first ability: giving space for our emotions (to feel what we feel) while not enmeshing ourselves with them. That is a mouthful. What do I mean? The author and Catholic priest Anthony De Mello described it beautifully when he said that our emotions are a weather pattern going across the expansive sky.[1]

It's as if I am the sky. So the anger, sadness, or fear I am feeling is not the whole of me. It does not make up the entirety of my being. I can feel it fully. It can be a raging thunderstorm. But even the biggest clouds are still just a fraction of the whole. How do we practically shift toward understanding that we are more than our current emotion?

We shift our language from "I am" to "I am experiencing." So instead of, "I am afraid," I can say, "I am experiencing fear." This might seem like a small change, but inwardly it has profound impact. If I am what I'm feeling, then I am caught up fully in the moment-to-moment storm. I am being tossed about (see Eph. 4:14). If I can acknowledge what I am feeling without the shame of having to identify fully with it—to look at it as something I am experiencing but not something I am—I have space to breathe and see more clearly.

———————

Practice: I Am Experiencing ...

1. Get still in a quiet place where you can be alone for a few minutes.
2. Connect with a feeling that feels large right now.
3. Say to yourself, "I am _____." Say it quietly to yourself a few times, then speak it out loud. What do you notice as you say this out loud?
4. Now try saying, "I am experiencing_____." Say it quietly to yourself a few times, then speak it out loud. Did you notice the shift in your inner experience? Could you feel the slight distance this created between you and the big feeling? It can feel like a switch between being *in* a movie and watching a movie. You gain enough space to see.
5. Take a breath of acceptance. It's okay to be experiencing this emotion. It is *not* all of you. Can you allow yourself to simply experience this?
6. Write down what you experienced. Try to describe the internal shift. Capture a bit of the learning. There is something tangible about writing down

an internal experience like this that makes it more concrete, and easier to build on later. If you give this a try and don't notice any shift at all, that's okay. Try it again over the next few days with a sense of patience and self-compassion. See if it changes anything for you.

———————

Chapter 3

Shift Work

To see a truth, to know what it is,
to understand it, and to love it, are all one.

George MacDonald, *Unspoken Sermons*

"Granny! Granny!" My son, Raylan, sprints through the house shrieking at the top of his lungs. He seems part joyful and part terrified. He'd just gone upstairs, a brave move for him. But now he's running down so, so scared. Because Granny almost got him.

Granny is a YouTube character who horrifies my son. She is part of a low-budget green-screen video that somehow has millions of views. He has seen it only once, but he talks about it incessantly. And sometimes he screams "Granny!" scaring himself and his (at that time) three-year-old sister, Penelope.

Raylan has autism. There are a lot of nuances to that, but part of it means he gets fixated on certain ideas or stories. Granny is officially in the *fixated* category. She haunts his waking hours and stalks his dreams. In fact, every night he asks me to pray for him—not for protection, not for good things to happen the next day, or even for other people—but for no dreams. Not even good dreams, as if he can't take any chances. Granny might show up in a good dream just as easily as a bad one, so he would rather have zero dreams. Just white-noise, sound-machine sleep.

"Okay," I say, and every night, I pray that prayer. I hold Raylan's hand or put my hand delicately on his arm so he feels connection but doesn't get overwhelmed and start to stim* (which right now involves screaming at the top of his lungs while jumping up and down).

So Granny has become a major part of our lives. This is unfortunate for Tiff and me, as it has made it so that alone time is not a thing for us. My son has to be around one of us at all times. He won't even go into his bedroom by himself in the middle of the day.

He saw this video only once, mind you. A boy from down the block showed it to him. Thanks for that.

In about month six of this obsession, we were testing out a new babysitter. She seemed great with the kids, and she accepted all of Raylan's unique traits with no judgment. We really liked that.

On her first night, we gave her the usual rules and guidelines. Here is the safety plan (including *Doc McStuffins* on the iPad for Penelope). Here is the list of phone numbers. Here is the bedtime routine. General stuff, but with an added layer for autism.

When we got home hours later, she looked concerned.

Expecting to hear about Raylan having a hard time or maybe breaking something, we steeled ourselves for the bad news. We have lost many babysitters over the years.

---

*   Stimming—a.k.a. self-stimulation—is a series of physical motions that helps a child calm down.

She whispered, "So, something happened upstairs." Her eyes pointed in that direction in a delicate motion, as if she didn't want to draw too much attention our way.

Tiff and I leaned in, breath held.

She lowered her voice even more. "Has Raylan ever talked to you about being sensitive to spirits?" Confused, we just looked at each other for a second. She went on. "Upstairs, he kept talking about an old woman, as if she was there in the room with us. I got goose bumps. The room felt weird, and I wasn't sure what was going on."

"What do you mean?" Tiffany asked.

"Does Raylan ever talk about the spirit of someone who passed here in the house? Someone he feels somehow? He calls her *Granny*."

At this point, we could barely hold it together. We didn't want to be rude or in any way shame the babysitter. But, no, Raylan does not have special spirit sensors. He has a YouTube video obsession.

God gives us these little bubbles of laughter that float to the surface, lifting us just enough to get us through each day. Maybe.

But the reality is that Raylan's fear of this YouTube character—whom he was never supposed to see in the first place—still affects his sleep. In fact, sleep has become our Mt. Everest. And, unfortunately, there are no elevators to the top.

Raylan stopped sleeping through the night when he was two and a half. It was December 2014. This was way before he'd encountered Granny. He would sleep only a handful of hours, and when he was awake, one of us had to be with him in order to make him feel safe. Medical sleep studies revealed that he needed surgery to clear his airway. I remember him in those tiny pajamas being carted away from us as the anesthesia took hold. We were trepidatious but hopeful.

Two months after that, we are back for a follow-up sleep study in the clinic. Raylan wakes up at 2:00 a.m., wide awake and ready for the day. The medical team sends us home. Later, his doctor calls. "Good news: His oxygen levels look great!"

We are excited but confused. We ask why, if the airway issue is fixed, he still isn't sleeping through the night. The doctor says it might have something to do with his other challenges. We have come to learn that "other challenges" is sometimes code for "I don't know" or "That is not my area of specialty."

There is a reason that sleep deprivation is part of the standard torture package. Your body and brain need sleep to reset and to recalibrate for the next day. When you don't sleep regularly for months and years at a time, you begin to feel physically and mentally brittle.

While Raylan seemed to function with only a few hours of sleep per night, I could not. And my ability to keep myself together was starting to fray at the edges. My whole life, I'd learned to do one thing: Suppress. Stuff it. "Just keep swimming," Dory style. This meant I was really good at hurrying up and doing the next thing. What I didn't know was that every time I stuffed or suppressed, I was getting further away from myself.

I was in pain, but I was tuning out that pain.

Six weeks after trauma camp, I was still not sleeping regularly. Raylan was older than he'd been in the Granny days, and the nights were not as bad as they had been. Back then, it was nonstop deprivation, and we got only about half of what we needed. The bags under my eyes were so large they could no longer be considered carry-ons.

One of the unique features of our sleep rhythm was that no matter what time Raylan woke up, it was always with the same incredibly loud bellow: "DAAAAAAADDDDDDYYYYYYYYY!" Emerging from whatever shallow semblance of sleep I'd been in, I would instantly be up. Heart racing, feet tiptoeing hurriedly toward his room. It felt really important to get there fast so his screaming would stop and Penelope and Tiff could stay asleep.

Internally, my body was releasing an overload of cortisol, more commonly known as the stress hormone. Which, according to a recent scientific journal, causes "pupillary dilation, increased heart rate and myocardial contractility, increased respiratory rate, diverted blood flow to organs vital to the fight or flight response."[1] Did you catch that? Stress is not just an idea or a mental construct. My eyes, heart, lungs, blood flow, and even other unnamed *vital* organs were going on high alert.

What this practically means is that my body, from the moment my feet hit the floor—every single day—was flooded with stress. There is even recent scientific research about something called the allostatic load, which refers to what happens to you when you are in chronic high stress and don't get to down-regulate your system very often.

"Down-regulate" is a fancy term for *chill*. According to the National Institutes of Health, "Allostatic load can significantly affect the aging process and result in reduced longevity, accelerated aging, and impaired health."[2] Sweet.

You and I probably haven't met yet, but if we were to meet one day, I think you'd notice—in addition to my missing molar—that my hair is almost all silver, verging on arctic white. And I'm not that old. (Actually, I hope you wouldn't notice the molar, since it is waaayyy back there.)

When your morning starts like this day after day, year after year, the wear and tear on your system begins to show. But this was not the most concerning thing to me. What I noticed in those first few weeks after trauma camp was that my stress level, which spiked in the morning, never fully went back down. I carried that intensity throughout my day.

Right now, as you're reading this, stand up quickly, hold your breath, and open your eyes wide while lifting your shoulders as high as they can go. Really get the tightness dialed into your neck area. That's what this kind of ongoing stress feels like.

I went to work every day bringing that with me. Shoulders so tight they were nearly touching my ears. I went to church with breath so shallow it felt like I was panting. All day, I would go from one thing to another, never starting in peace, let alone returning to peace. Prior to trauma camp, I was convinced that this was just the way my life was.

Now, however, I heard the gentle pull of the Spirit calling me to something different. But what?

The Shift to Curiosity

The first thing that had to change in me was that I had to develop a willingness to get curious. Sounds simple, but this is a big deal. If I wanted a change from the stressful mornings, I was going to have to create something new.

I started with a blank sheet of paper.

Step 1: Ideate

I wrote "What would a joyful morning feel like?" across the top of it.

I used the word *feel* intentionally. I didn't want my rational, planning side to take over here. I wanted to gently explore from a different intelligence center.

Below the heading I wrote, with no self-judgment, these things:

- It would feel open.
- Creative.
- Hopeful.
- Inspiring.
- Light.
- Spacious.
- Exploratory.
- I would feel awe and wonder.
- It would feel like flow and *not* grind.
- I would feel loved.
- I would feel trusted and trusting.
- I would feel safe.
- My day would be full of kindnesses given and received.

I looked at the list and just let it settle. There was a part of me that instantly screamed, *This is not possible! Stop now! You are setting yourself up for disappointment, and you know it, you idiot.*

I kindly asked this part of me for a little space. To suspend its disbelief and embrace a bit of emotional risk.

Step 2: Design

My next heading: "What tasks or activities would support this kind of morning?"

I love lists, checkboxes, and calendars. I love to make a plan, stick to the plan, and then reap the long-term benefits of said plan. All while feeling slightly superior.

So it was important to me that I didn't simply stay in the land of theory. While it might be nice to imagine a joyful day, at this point it was a theoretical thing, an emotional version of quantum physics that might not be obtainable for a mere mortal like me. It had to be real.

Below that second heading, I listed things quickly, as if they bubbled up from my subconscious. Every morning would be incredible. How?

- I would wake up on my own, an hour before Raylan yelling.
- I would have a quiet hour.
- I would pray in this hour.
- I would practice breath work in this hour.
- I would meditate on wisdom in this hour. Wisdom from Scripture and ancient wisdom from the saints and mystics.

- I would journal.
- Sometimes I might even do yoga. (I wasn't good at yoga, but at that hour, no one in my house would see me if I fell.)
- I would move toward every member in my family with the goal of being heart-connected.
- I would recognize that they don't have to receive my attempts at heart connection. And I would not hold it against them if they weren't up for it.
- I would run while listening to good music. Sometimes worship stuff; sometimes U2, Jon Batiste, and Huey Lewis and the News. No judgment. Sometimes I would run with no music at all and just dance and pray. And yes, dance running is a thing.

I stopped writing and looked at the list. This seemed like a dream morning. Was it possible? Could anyone with small kids have this kind of morning, let alone someone with a child with disabilities? Could I do this in a way that Tiff would feel deeply loved, seen, and cared for? I wasn't sure. But I was committed to finding out.

Step 3: Implement

A good action plan needs action. Seems obvious, but the world (like my life) is full of good ideas that never see daylight due to the inability or the failure to implement them. But this vision of a new morning, a joyful morning, was so compelling that I couldn't let it go. I had to see if I could actually get it off the ground.

I took out a new sheet of paper and wrote: "What would I need to pull this off?"

- Eight hours of sleep—so go to bed earlier.
  - What time? 8:30 p.m. (ish).
- I will need to wake up earlier than Raylan on an average basis. Most days, he wakes up at 5:45. Okay, wake up at 4:45.
- A reliable alarm that won't wake Tiff up. My watch has a handy vibration feature that will do that well.
- I need a coffee maker in our bedroom. Why? Because if I leave the room, Raylan will wake up.
  - Use the single-cup Keurig K-Cup maker I got for Christmas. The coffee will be quick and full of caffeine.
- I need a comfortable chair to sit in to pray, meditate, and do breath work.
  - Ask Tiff if I can borrow the one from the living room that no one currently uses except the dog.

I took this plan to Tiff to see how she felt about it. She was on board with me taking the chair but on one condition: Would I take point on the kids when they did wake up and get them ready for school? Including homework with Penelope? Of course. She gave me permission to steal the chair from the living room, and she even went so far as to find a little desk on Facebook Marketplace in case I wanted to write. She was investing in this vision with me.

Tiff and I added one more element to this morning routine: a simple moment of blessing for each other. After my hour, I would wake her up with a fresh cup of coffee (with creamer of her choice). When I did this, I would share one thing I was grateful for that had happened in the last twenty-four hours. This had to be real. This couldn't be some nonsense greeting-card thing I didn't actually feel.

She would sit up in bed. We'd have this moment. She would share something she was grateful for about me, as well. It was tender, occasionally awkward, and vulnerable in the best kind of way.

This whole "redesign my morning" process started with a willingness to shift into curiosity. This switch took about a week. Just one week to change a pattern that had been eating my lunch for years.

Most mornings, Raylan woke up at about 5:45. So I began waking up at 4:45—refreshed, since I had gone to bed so early. I made my cup of coffee in the dark, got comfortable in my prayer chair, and sat silently before the Lord.

I can't emphasize enough that this was (and is) pure joy. It did not feel like "discipline." Remember, I started this whole process with joy front and center. How would I have a joyful morning, given my context? And so it turned out.

Then, after time praying, reading, meditating, breathing, and bad yoga, when Raylan began to holler "DAAAADDDDYYYYYY!!!!!" there was no cortisol flooding. I just walked into his room. Often, I'd lie down with him. I could be a calming presence because I was actually calm.

Not only was my morning different, but the whole day shifted. I wasn't playing catch-up anymore, digging myself out of a stress hole the size of the Grand Canyon.

Now, if you are thinking, *Must be nice for you*, let me say that you are correct—it is nice for me. And I don't know what would be nice for you. Only you know that. If you want to stay where you are, stay. But if you'd like to see some actual changes, a move toward slightly more joy, try shifting to curiosity.

PRACTICE: A Day of Joy

Now it's your turn. Grab a fresh sheet of paper—or create a blank word processing document, if that is more your style. Write "What would a joyful day feel like?" across the top.

1. Write out your answer. Insert sections for morning, afternoon, evening, night, wee hours, or whatever time you need to focus on. I started with early morning, but you might have another part of the day that needs your attention.

2. What tasks or activities would support this kind of day?

3. What would you need in order to pull this off? Do you need a chair and a Keurig K-Cup coffee maker like I did? (By the way, Keurig is not sponsoring this book, but I'm available as a brand ambassador.)

4. Practice the day. Actually try it on. See how it feels. Does anything need to change or be adjusted?

Before we leave this redesigned morning, I'd like to invite you into a closer look at a few of the rhythms that changed my experience. The first is a critical idea we will come back to again and again: awareness.

Awareness

What the desert fathers—the monastics—called contemplative prayer or simply contemplation, I am calling Spirit-led self-awareness. It is intentional inward awareness, self-observation (note that this is very different from self-absorption). It is Spirit-led observation. It is learning to sit still and notice the ways of the Lord working on your innermost being. Thomas Merton wrote:

> We must face the fact that the mere thought of contemplation is one which deeply troubles the person who takes it seriously. It is so contrary to the modern way of life, so apparently alien, so seemingly impossible, that the modern man who even considers it finds, at first, that his whole being rebels against it. If the ideal of inner peace remains attractive, the demands of the way to peace seem to be so exacting and extreme that they can no longer be met. We would like to be quiet, but our restlessness will not allow it.[3]

So how do we get there? Slowly, and with much grace for ourselves. This way is not grasping with a demanding hand, impatient at our progress. But rather this way requires a spirit of creativity and joy, playful like a child running to Jesus. Scripture gives us two great examples of this.

When James and John, two of Jesus' disciples, try to get Jesus to confirm them as His right and left hands of power, this is grasping, demanding. In fact, Jesus tells them directly that this is *not* the way. He said that they were still trying to control an outcome (see Matt. 20:20–28).

Contrast this with the example of the children who simply run to Jesus, and He holds them up as examples of true kingdom participants (see Mark 10:13–16). He is showing us the way. The kids are not evaluating their performance. They are not jockeying for position or trying to control the outcome. They simply love being near the giver of all life, and He loves being near them. They play in His presence, at peace and feeling wonder with the world He created.

In a sense, this was the space I carved out in that chair. I got still. I got present. I learned to breathe. I urge you to do the same.

I remember the first time someone told me he was into breath work. I had no idea what he meant, so I nodded and waited for him to start talking about something else. Hopefully, something that was remotely interesting to me. I later found out what breath work actually was: intentional breathing exercises that have been shown to lower anxiety, heart rates, and blood pressure.

Still, I thought, *That sounds like some hippie nonsense.* I was at a marriage retreat, we were all in a circle, and someone was "guiding" us through a breathing exercise. I was so uncomfortable that I sweat through both my T-shirt and my sweatshirt. It was not a good look. So I did that thing I do when I have to do something I've already decided not to like: I didn't really try. And guess what—*it didn't work!*

I came away from that experience feeling a bit smug. I knew it wouldn't work, and sure enough, it didn't. But I also came away still really stressed out.

Sometime later, I came across the science behind it.[4] Research has repeatedly shown that breathing exercises done consistently lower stress, anxiety, and even symptoms of depression.

I read about how our sympathetic nervous system—the fight, flight, or freeze part of us—is really good at protecting us but not very good at discerning when something is a bear or just an upset boss. It turns out that breath work helps tell the sympathetic nervous system that it can relax. It's a way to communicate "You are safe" to this hair-trigger part of us. Some researchers are finding that consistent breath work can possibly get you out of stuck patterns of thinking and behavior, literally giving the brain an easier path toward increased neuroplasticity.[5] All this from simple breathing.

The next time I came across breath work was at the trauma retreat center. Little did I know what breakthroughs awaited me. This time when someone wanted to lead me through breath work, I was willing to give it an honest try.

Lo and behold, as my breathing slowed and got deep into my belly, my heart rate slowed. My shoulders began to drop. The tension in my jaw eased just a touch. I found myself a bit more open to the possibility that this trauma center might have something for me. I slowly moved from closed to open.

Years later, I still do breath work every day. For me, that is always early in the morning, then again when I arrive in the office to move into work mode, and often before bed.

Below is a simple practice to get you going. If you're ready for your pain to stop, let's start something new.

Practice: 4x4 Breathing

1. Sit down, get comfortable. For me, that means sitting in a simple chair with my feet firmly planted on the floor or ground. Kick off your shoes if that feels good.

2. Be in a space where you won't be interrupted for about five minutes. As I've said, I moved a chair into my bedroom to create that space (and installed a new lock on my door that my kids couldn't pick; true story). I use noise-canceling headphones and some meditation music, but you should go with whatever helps you tune out the world around you.

3. Start with an intake of breath. Breathe in while counting to four in your head.

4. Exhale while counting to four.

5. Do this again.

6. And again.

7. And finally, one last time.

This is a simple 4x4. In that little bit of time, your breathing has slowed, your heart rate has slowed, and you will likely be just a bit more dialed into what you are feeling. Way to go!

———————

Chapter 4

Reconnecting with Dad

We read the Gospels not merely to get a picture or
an idea of Christ but to enter in and pass through the
words of revelation to establish, by faith, a vital contact
with the Christ Who dwells in our souls as God.

Thomas Merton, *New Seeds of Contemplation*

It is early spring and I am just starting to imagine what warmth will feel like again. It has been a long winter. Things are changing outside. The birds are back. The trees are starting to bud. There is a literal thawing that serves as a sharp contrast to what is happening in our home. Tiff seems to be sliding into a new round of acute depression. Her Complex PTSD seems intent on taking her out.

Meanwhile, our son is struggling in school. We have kept him in the public system this whole time for a few reasons. Originally, this was a sense of civic duty. If we wanted to see our public schools get better, we felt we couldn't just take our children out of them. We needed to invest there ourselves.

We love his school. We love the teachers. But they can't give him enough of what he needs. It is a dosage problem. If you told me you had migraines and I gave you three ibuprofen a month, you would have one good afternoon. Maybe. Raylan couldn't get the one-on-one aid he needed to make school doable.

The school challenges are turning into a daily anxiety for him that has become unmanageable. He does not know how to tell us verbally what he is feeling. But he does communicate through broken toys, chairs, bowls, and televisions.

Breaking TV screens has become a particular favorite as they seem to give him a bit of sensory joy in the way they crack like spiderwebs. The first time he breaks one, newly installed from a Costco Saturday that got away from me, I think, *Okay, but he won't do that again.* When he cracks the next one, we begin looking on Facebook Marketplace for flat-screen-adjacent models for ten dollars. We go through these quickly too. Eventually, I handcraft a plexiglass protection shield. But I'm not handy, so it keeps falling off. Who knew it was so hard to superglue plexiglass?

The intensity all comes to a head one day when we are at the children's hospital. We have a medical team waiting for us on the ninth floor. I pull the car into the valet parking section, which you learn about if you come here often. The staff have the kindest eyes of any valets in the country. Some of the doctors I've worked with don't have the bedside manner of these amazing people.

Right away, they notice that things seem challenging in our van. Raylan is screaming and doesn't want to be here. I don't want to be here. Tiff, silently crying, does not want to be here either. We are all in intense emotional pain. Raylan has slid down to the bottom of the seat, not really in it anymore but sort of suspended from the seat belt. We try to gently untangle him while not touching him. Touching him lightly when he is in this mental/physical space is a recipe for disaster. We Jenga-style take him out of the van.

At first, he walks with us across the connecting bridge into the main lobby. Tiff and I are holding our breath. My body feels so tight. We make it past the check-in desk, and the elevator doors open. We made it!

Nope. The elevator is full already. I see the confusion on Raylan's face. Tiff explains that we are going to wait for the next one. But that one is full too. At this point, Raylan begins screaming again. He throws himself on the hospital floor. The cleanest floor, really.

The elevator arrives, and this time it's only half full, so we decide to go for it. But Raylan is in full meltdown mode now. You know how everyone looks only at their phone or the numbers above the elevator? That stops. Everyone is looking at us. People don't know what to do. We try to pick Raylan up, but this only makes it worse. He is now kicking uncontrollably and tries to spit at everyone and everything near him. He is, in fact, spitting mad.

We are eventually able to prop him up between us and walk him into the elevator. No one else gets on with us. They all have this same look on their face: one part grimace and one part judgment. Apparently, we are the worst parents in the children's hospital this day.

When we get off on the ninth floor, I stay with Raylan while Tiff rushes over to the nurses' station to explain the situation. But we feel relief: We are on the ninth floor, the floor with the experts. They will know what to do.

Meanwhile, Raylan is still in full sensory meltdown. Several nurses come out but just stand there in shock. I ask, "Can you help me get him to the appointment room?" I am sweating from effort and anxiety. They don't seem to know what to do besides pointing us in the general direction of the appointment room.

Along the way, walls are kicked. Shoes come off. Tiff is not so silently crying anymore. My face is turning a shade of red not found in nature. At long last, we get to the room, and soon two of our doctors come in.

Tiff is on the floor holding Raylan. Her tenderness reminds me of some sort of pietà painting of the Virgin Mary with the not-yet-resurrected body of Jesus.

We are doing our best. This is so, so hard.

I feel hope now that the doctors are here. I feel anticipation, like they are going to explain a thing or two that will unlock this moment for us. This is not what happens.

They each take a seat, and the first doctor gently explains that today has been very informative. I look at her quizzically. She says, somewhat nervously, "I mean, this shows us that our nursing staff requires more training for this level of care."

I say, "Aren't you the best-trained resources in the state?"

She looks at her colleague sheepishly. "Yes."

"So are you saying that we have one of the most complicated cases you've seen?"

She opens her hands. "This is more of an intense situation than we deal with regularly." The look on her face already tells me that they have few answers for us.

I make a joke about getting a T-shirt that says "We are number one." In a way, though, I feel validated. This really is hard, if the professionals are pushed beyond their ability. I also feel a wave of hopelessness. If the best medical people in our city don't have good answers for us, then what do we do?

Like so many days after visiting loving and well-intentioned medical professionals, that day we went home exhausted and with no clear plan.

Going home was a theme for me in this season.

At trauma camp, through intentional work to connect with the core of who I am, I began to return to myself. To who I was before the world had gotten hold of me and before I had gotten hold of the world. It was a feeling akin to something out of the prodigal son story: *"But when he came to himself,* he said, 'How many of my father's hired servants have more than enough bread, but I perish here with hunger!'"* (Luke 15:17). It was one part revelation, one part remembering something long forgotten but always known, and one part simple homecoming.

After this experience, I wanted to connect with my faith from a different starting point. Realizing I had some internal unwinding to do, which had really just begun, I determined to look anew at Scripture. And to do so not just through fresh eyes but also in a new manner.

I realized that up until this point I had come to the Word to pin God down. To learn all the facts and figures of the divine so I might get a grasp on Him. A firm grip ... an under-my-control grip. (Better known as idolatry.) Like a scientist studying butterflies* who was not content to watch them fly, I had to capture them, put them in a box, and stop their movement so I could observe them the way I wanted to observe. As if I had to unmake the butterfly to learn the butterfly. I made the pursuit of the Lord clinical, and in so doing drained the life right out of what should've been a life-giving relationship.

Now, I would not have told you this out loud. But this tendency to want to control things and people was nothing new. It existed in all other parts of my life. To me, to know God was to box Him in, limit Him, draw Him in smaller lines so that my mind could encompass the unending one.

In short, I wanted to put limits on a God defined by limitless love, mercy, kindness, justice, strength, and power.

But having seen this thread throughout my life, and becoming aware of how it limited and hurt me and those around me, I determined to read Scripture differently. The place I decided to start was the parable of the prodigal son (Luke 15:11–32). I determined to read just this story for an entire year.

Why this story? My attempt to have a controlling grip on God came from my own mental image of Him as a demanding and distant father who gave grace but demanded performance. Like most of us (if not *all* of us), part of my understanding of my heavenly Father was drawn from my earthly parents. Now, my parents are remarkable people who loved me and my siblings well, but of course they also

---

*   This person is called a lepidopterist, by the way. I looked it up to save you the time.

had their own lenses and generational blessings and curses that had shaped them.

One of these influences was the voice of a family member who had an outsized power and presence. To this person, God was good, but He wanted you to get it *right*. And you could get it *right*. And if you weren't getting it *right*, you weren't trying hard enough. The one thing to get you moving? Shame. This laid a foundation for a performance-based faith.

This family member was rumored to have said, "We are better than other people because we are Christians, and we are better than other Christians because we are Southern Baptists." Now, I never heard this person say this. But we *felt* this as a family.

But there is no performance in the prodigal son story. I have come to believe that this parable encompasses the great emotional truth of the gospel of Jesus Christ: we are fully known and fully loved by the God who lovingly made us. As I read this story over and over again, it reshaped my heart and mind. It taught me how to draw near to that heart of love and to find it in my own inner self. I learned how to move and have my being in the love of the Father and how to engage with those around me from that core of love.

The aha moment for me was Luke 15:17. The prodigal son finds himself miserable and far from home:

> He was longing to be fed with the pods that the pigs
> ate, and no one gave him anything. *But when he came*
> *to himself,* he said, "How many of my father's hired
> servants have more than enough bread, but I perish

here with hunger! I will arise and go to my father."
(Luke 15:16–18a)

"But when he came to himself." I love that phrase. Some other
translations say, "But when he came to his senses." It's as if, in a moment
of Spirit-given clarity, he remembered who he was. Not who he was
trying to be in this foreign land but who he was at his core. With this
realization came a beautiful awareness of what he needed to do: he had
to go home. There was no other place to be *but* home with his father.
This was his truest self.

Yet on his journey back, he got caught up in the shame spiral. A
spiral that all of us, if we are honest for a minute, can relate to. It goes
like this:

- I don't deserve to be His son anymore.
- The most I can hope for is to be His servant.
- I must grovel to earn a not-so-great place back at
  home.

He automatically put a limit on the possibilities of his father's love.
It simply couldn't be that good. The young man was limping home,
dripping shame, and desperately hungry. Have you ever tried to take a
long walk when you are hungry? It's the worst.

When his father saw him approaching on the road, he didn't do
any of the things we would expect an earthly father to do or say, such as:

- "Well, look who couldn't cut it in the big city. Told
  you so."

- "Do you know how much worry you have caused your mom and me?"
- "What is your repayment plan on all that money you lost?"
- "I am so disappointed."

What words does the voice of shame use in your life?

One of the things that comes with a commitment to the journey of Spirit-led self-awareness is that you start to learn how you were shaped by shame stories. You'll identify the stories that got really big and stayed really big. And the ones that are still shaping your heart.

One of the biggest for me was the day I almost bought a gun. I was twelve.

I went to a fairly rough junior high school. So much so that having a gun seemed like a necessary safety precaution. This was not mere fantasy. I knew who would sell me a gun, where and how to meet up with him, and roughly what it would cost.

In my school, there was a kid who had stayed back so many times, he had a mustache. He was still in seventh grade. Rumor had it that he drove himself to school on occasion, though I could never verify this. Let's call him Larry, and after one particular school dance near the end of my eighth-grade year, he started telling people that he was going to kill me. Apparently, I had gotten too close to his girlfriend on the dance floor.

Now, this would be laughable in a school environment not filled with violence. But I had personally seen this kid and his friends jump another kid after school. Kicking his head into the concrete and cracking his ribs as they stomped on him. Still, childhood memories can be exaggerated. So I recently asked one of my brothers who had also attended the school if it had been as bad as I remembered. He said he had never been more afraid in his life.

So now I've got a known violent student saying he's going to kill me. While I was getting up the courage to buy the gun, I approached my dad to get his advice. He was sitting in his blue La-Z-Boy chair in the corner of the living room reading a book. I framed the question, as one does, through a hypothetical friend. "Hey, Dad, a friend of mine is thinking about buying a gun. What should I tell him?"

My dad put the book down and took off his reading glasses. His jaw pulsed. Of course, he saw right through me. "Will," he said in an angry tone shaped by judgment, "if that is what you are going to do, then you need to go to school tomorrow and tell everyone that you are *not* a Christian anymore!" He was so mad.

I think I flinched. I'm not sure. I know I screamed back, calling him a word not fit for prime-time television. That was the first and only time I ever swore at my dad. I ran back to my room and essentially grounded myself.

What had I wanted to happen? I'd wanted my dad to see my fear. It has been decades, but I can still recall the metallic taste of that fear. It is just right there. It feels somehow settled into my bones, like the violence will eventually find me, inevitably. I wanted him to see that first and foremost. Not the potential for me to make a dumb decision with awful ramifications. I wanted him to wrap me in his arms and say, "Oh, buddy, I am so sorry you are this scared. What is happening at this school? I've got you. You are okay now."

I didn't buy the gun.

Right at the end of eighth grade, everything came to a head with Larry. It was supposed to be the eighth-grade graduation ceremony, but I knew that after the bell rang, I was going to be the kid getting his head kicked into the wall. Everyone was talking about it. My friends were scared for me but not willing to do anything to intervene. Snitches get stitches and whatnot.

I decided to deal with this problem head-on and take responsibility. With my heart rate at 150 bmp and my fear so large it had left the pit of my stomach and taken over my entire torso, I went striding down the seventh-grade hall and found Larry in his classroom. It was art class, and the teacher, Mr. Carter, walked out right as I walked in. I wanted him to stop me, to ask what was going on, but he didn't. He said hi and kept walking to the bathroom.

I walked over to Larry and tried to explain that I hadn't danced with his girlfriend. He jumped out of his chair, knocking it over. I actually saw fear in his eyes that I had shown up like this. And then I saw the moment when he shifted into predator mode. His scowl was huge. His words were conjugations of swears never before heard in Mr. Carter's art class. He started bumping my chest, leaning so close that his mustache stood over me. This was not going well.

Apparently, the yelling was loud enough to call Mr. Carter back into the room. He broke us apart and kicked me out of his class. But he did nothing else. I was alone in the hallway wishing someone would protect me. In a few minutes, I was supposed to go downstairs and walk across the stage with the other eighth graders. I was supposed to get encouraging messages written in our thin, softbound yearbook. Instead, wiping tears from my eyes, I opened an emergency exit door and left.

No alarm sounded. No one followed me. I ran all the way home before Larry could grab his crew.

That whole summer, I stayed within the few blocks around my house where I could be sure I wouldn't run into him. The next year, I went to a high school farther in the suburbs. I would never have to see Larry again.

This was the story that had to get dismantled before I could receive the love of my heavenly Father. It was as if I had to have God take apart this childhood moment that had shaped me so much.

Anytime I got to the part in the prodigal son story where the father runs out and wraps his son in love, some part of me froze up. The father whispers love in his son's ear and doesn't shame him. Instead, he essentially says, "Hear that sound? That is the band warming up for your homecoming party. It is going to be incredible!" But because of my own story, I believed God's love could not be that good. Impossible.

Eventually, through the working of the Spirit and the Word, I called my dad. I asked if he was willing to go through that painful moment with me. I wasn't even sure he would remember. He did.

He listened. He held space. He received my vulnerability in the best way possible, with his own vulnerability. He didn't get defensive or rationalize. Instead, he said, "Oh, Will, I am so sorry. I think at that time it mattered so much to me that our whole family looked like really good Christians. I think I was afraid of what would happen to the church and the ministry if that started to unravel."

There was a small part of me that was holding its breath until this conversation. A tension just below the surface. That day on the phone, my dad gave me a tremendous gift: his full presence.

With full presence comes forgiveness, healing, wholeness.

PRACTICE: A New Way of Reading

When I became aware I needed to engage with Scripture in a new way, I wasn't sure what that would look like. But I trusted the Lord would meet me in that space and know how to lead me forward. So the first part of this practice is just to hold a willingness to be met by the Lord in the Word.

As I read the prodigal son story over and over again, there arose a temptation to make it a checkbox or a duty. I noticed this when it happened, and I decided to get curious. Why do I want to make this a duty? What do I think I am earning (or not earning) if I engage in this with a duty-bound heart? Each time that came up, I simply noticed, got curious, and journaled. If you notice something similar during this practice, hold space for curiosity.

Finally, I allowed myself to fully engage my imagination with the story. I stepped into it, breathed it, lived it—and, most importantly, felt it. Stories are empathy vehicles. They are meant to grab hold of our hearts and take us on an emotional journey. Jesus loved stories. Some have speculated on why it was one of His primary modes of communication. I think it is simple: Jesus knew that stories were the key to people's hearts. They were the shortcut, the cheat code, the hack that moved His listeners to the right emotional and spiritual place to experience life change. Stories are the plow of the heart, preparing the ground for new seeds.

Here is a guide to do this for yourself:

1. Get still. Find a place where you will not be disturbed. Give yourself fifteen minutes at least.
2. Breathe. Calm your body.
3. Read the story of the prodigal son once through (Luke 15:11–32). Just notice what you notice.
4. Close your eyes and retell the story to yourself. As you do this, notice what comes up for you. Draw the spotlight of your awareness toward any emotional reactions. For instance, I got mad at the son for leaving. How dare he do that to his loving dad! If something like this comes up, write it out, journal, explore, get curious. Ask, "Why do I feel this so strongly?"
5. Step into the story. Imagine yourself in the role of the prodigal son. What comes up for you? Shift into the role of the older brother. What is his driving motivation? What do you feel when you step from the darkness and hear the music at the house? Step into the role of the father. What is it like to embrace the child whom you believed to be dead but is now safely home?

When we read Scripture like this, we are no longer coming to the text simply for intellectual information, as if preparing for an exam. We are instead breathing with and through the life-giving presence of the Spirit. The story gets a heartbeat again.

If this is hard for you at first, that's okay. Don't let this be another source of self-condemnation. Instead, stay in play mode. God, your Father, delights in you and is inviting you into life change even now. You won't go too slow for Him. He will not leave you behind. He has you fully embraced. You are safe. You are loved.

———————

Chapter 5

All the Drama

True homecoming is choosing the way of Jesus, where we
acknowledge the good and painful in our lives and we ask for
patience and courage to forgive all those who have wounded
us on the journey. Their love was limited and conditional, but
it set us in search of that unconditional, unlimited love.

Henri Nouwen, *The Return of the Prodigal Son*

I always dread the approach of summer as a parent. On it comes, like
an anxiety train barreling toward our house. Families affected by disabilities often have to scramble during the summer. Services provided
through the school system are canceled, and other therapies have such
limited hours that they stop being of much use. Every summer, we try
all the things to make it work. And we end every summer feeling as if
we've just finished an ultramarathon in the desert.[1]

One year recently, Tiffany and I were looking at the summer
schedule in white-knuckled fear. It was that moment when you shift
from vague unease to an elevated heart rate. This was not paranoia

but a reasonable response to what we'd experienced before: summer after summer of barely surviving. When you've had consistently hard experiences, you predict more hard experiences.

This type of thinking is sometimes described as the *default future.*[2] It's the belief that tomorrow holds more of what yesterday held. Now, having done a lot of self-awareness work, I understood what was happening. But I didn't quite know what to do about it.

The worst of these summers happened in the midst of COVID-19. Like everyone else, we had been home all spring. It was as if the dreaded summer had come early. Remote learning had zero chance at meeting the needs of our son, so every day felt like a choose-your-own-adventure story that ended with us being eaten by a shark.

Don't get me wrong: Our son is amazing, and we always want to give him everything he needs to thrive. He is an incredible kid who loves basketball, football, his friends, and sneakers. Did I mention he is a sneakerhead?

But this summer, after day upon day and hour upon hour of nonstop intensity, I noticed myself shifting into project-management mode. I began to feel, at a heart level, like my son was a problem to solve. Worse, I began to act like it.

There was one week where he kicked out two large glass panels while wearing only socks on his feet. After the first panel, he was fine. No cuts, and no hospital needed. He was less fortunate on the second one. His little foot needed eight stitches. Remember, this was a time when the authorities were recommending we wipe down our groceries with Clorox. To go to the ER for stitches felt like jumping off a medical cliff without knowing what was at the bottom. We were sad, we were weary, and we were scared.

Our medical team weighed in from a distance, but the first recommendation our doctor gave us was, "It may be time to get him residential care." This was code for institutionalizing him. However, even if we'd wanted to do that (which of course we didn't), with his young age and the global pandemic raging around us, the only options were out of state. Also, each place required the kind of money that only an A-list celebrity or hedge fund manager could pull off. We'd been downwardly mobile for a while, launching a nonprofit. Aghast, I asked her, "Is there no plan B?"

She paused. "Well, you could get him significant in-home treatment, and we could try to get him into the best psychiatrist in town. Her wait list is usually about six months."

Tiff and I looked at each other. "What does in-home treatment look like?" I asked.

"I think you'd start with thirty hours a week of therapy in the house with someone with the right credentials. Once you see some improvement, you could lower it to twenty hours a week."

"Is any of that covered by insurance?" I asked, mentally logging into our checking account.

"Not typically, Mr. Acuff."

Tiff leaned toward the camera. "How about the psychiatrist you mentioned. Is that covered?"

The doctor smiled sadly. "No, she is just out of pocket."

I did the math. We were talking about twenty-five thousand dollars per *month.*

Did I mention we had just started a faith-based nonprofit? The nonprofit world is the only industry that promises *not* to make money.

We got off the phone and prayed. We didn't pray in some sort of triumphal way. We prayed like two really scared parents who didn't know how they were going to keep their family together.

In that most tender of places, God met us. He made a way where we saw no way.

Our nonprofit is centered on creating pathways of economic opportunity for underestimated neighbors so they can financially flourish on their own terms. One of our biggest programs is "The Academy," where we equip neighbors with the tools to plan, start, and grow their own small business. It just so happened that one of our graduates had exactly the credentials to do the in-home therapy our doctor recommended.

Her name is Shemicka, and she is one of God's saints. I called her and gave her the full rundown. All her other clients had canceled because of COVID. I asked her if she would be willing to come into our "COVID bubble" *and* reduce her normal rates. I didn't know where even the lesser amount of money would come from, but I was convinced that our friends, family, and neighbors would chip in to help keep our family together.

Shemicka said yes. She was at our house later that afternoon.

Then I started calling and texting my most generous and tender-hearted friends who had shown love to our family in the past. I told them the full story. These were breathy and desperate phone calls:

"The doctor is recommending residential care out of state, but we are convinced Raylan needs to remain in our home. There might come a day when he needs those kinds of services, but it is not today. Can you help?"

My Venmo notification started pinging. One incredibly generous person after another chipped in. Shemicka let me pay her twice a month. We did this for three months. Over and over again, right when the little Venmo indicator showed $0 in its bright blue font—*ping*. Someone would give. It felt like a little slice of the New Testament.

Then we got a breakthrough on the psychiatrist. She'd also had a ton of cancellations, and she said she could do telehealth with us in two weeks, and would we want that slot? We said yes, praising God for His mercy and rejoicing that technology had matured to a place where this could happen.

That summer, there were a million stories of love, mercy, and kindness when we didn't think we could go another day. We lived on the bleeding edge of trust. But this was before either of us had encountered trauma camp. We didn't have any self-awareness tools.

We didn't know that we were being nonstop flooded with stress and cortisol. We didn't know why Tiff was crashing more and more, retreating to the safety of sleep. I didn't know why I had started to treat my family like a work project, something to be managed but with less and less heart connection every day. To be honest, I don't think I even noticed that the heart connection was gone. I was just trying to survive.

This pattern became the new normal in our lives. The thing about having to fight for survival is that it becomes all-consuming. You never stop to investigate the fear—you just do the next thing. You never wonder why your skin feels paper-thin and your chest is constricted. You might notice that your muscles always feel tight, but you can't spare the time to investigate that data point.

Survival becomes a sort of self-fulfilling prophecy. It becomes a matter of, "I do this because I must do this, and life will always be like this, so I must keep doing this." Our summer had become some sort of *Groundhog Day* but a lot less funny.* In survival mode, there is no play. There is no humor. There is just the next thing that you hope will lead to more survival.

During this time, and quite without realizing it, I had begun to live like a victim. In the shift from loving dad to project manager, I had begun to blame my son for the hardships of my life. I would never say this out loud (because you would judge me and think I'm an awful dad), but I would *feel*, "This is your fault, son" and, "Why is this happening to me?"

There are all sorts of blogs, books, articles, and research papers about the victimhood mindset.[3] One concept that I have found especially helpful is the drama triangle, originally created by Dr. Stephen Karpman in 1968 as a social model designed to explain conflict in human behavior.[4] The basic idea is that there are three roles involved with the victim mindset: hero, villain, and victim.

The hero tries to temporarily lower their own negative feelings by being a rescuer. This means they must find (or create) someone who needs rescuing—and someone who is (or can be portrayed as) threatening the victim in some way.

The hero often meddles or takes on responsibility that is not theirs to bear. They try to save or fix someone who might or might not want to be saved or fixed. They gravitate to people who are willing to take on the victim role, and they usually can pull off their role as rescuer for a small window of time only. They need someone to feel weak around them in order to make them feel strong. They are excellent "peacefakers." This is not an effective way to live.

The villain blames (or is said to blame) the other person or thing they view as responsible and is often critical and controlling. The villain tends to lead with anger. "I can't believe you would do this to me, you idiot" is the vibe of the villain.

Finally, there is the victim. The drama triangle can be confusing because all three roles are technically victim mindsets. But one of the three is straight-up called the victim. The victim role argues strongly that they are utterly stuck, nothing can be done, there is no hope, and they are essentially at the mercy of circumstances. Those circumstances can change but their "stuckness" does not change. One day it is the economy, the next day it is the weather, the sick dog, or the IRS. The vibe is "It all sucks, so why try?"[5]

One of the most interesting things about the drama triangle is that we don't stay in one position. We tend to run the bases as in a dysfunctional game of baseball, sprinting from villain to hero to victim at dizzying speed.

For example, here is a pattern that used to be common in our house:

I come home from a long day at work, slightly hangry and wanting to step into a peaceful house. Instead, I see that my son is having a really hard time (screaming, yelling, throwing things), and Tiff is trying to help him calm down by taking him to his room to down-regulate. My daughter is on her iPad in her bedroom and out of the immediate vicinity of the intensity.

As a hero, I charge in, take over for Tiff, and try to hurry Raylan to his room. (Notice I am rushing him to a space to get calm. How will that work? Has rushing ever made you feel calm? I digress.) I don't understand that me taking on the role of hero is an assumption that Tiff is a victim in need of rescuing. I'm basically undercutting her own capabilities and declaring that she is weak and incapable.

Not surprisingly, Tiffany responds to my attempts to rescue her by asking, "What are you doing? I have this!" In her mind, she's resisting my victim-ification of her, but in my mind, she seems to take on the villain role and go on the offensive. Now I run from hero to victim and say, "I'm just trying to help! Why don't you get that and just say 'thank you'?" Now, at this point, Tiff, being an Enneagram eight, doubles down on what I perceive as villain and goes in for a stronger attack in order to convince me that I am actually to blame. Doesn't she understand that I'm the good guy here?

I hope that was as exhausting to read as it was to live.

Another common pattern for me was with Raylan. I rounded the bases on my own. He wasn't even playing the game. If he began to have a hard time, I would immediately try to be the hero in order to alleviate the anger or tension. If that didn't work, I would run to villain mode and internally blame him for how hard my life was. Then, after the dust of that particular moment had cleared, I would land on victim, telling myself that I could never be happy or fulfilled if we didn't get a handle on his challenges. This was a lie shaped by my victim mindset.

Another way of saying this is that I had ceded my own emotional well-being to a child who couldn't regulate his own emotions. When I say it like that, it is immediately apparent as ludicrous, right? Yet some of us do this all the time. We firmly believe that the only way we can be okay is if someone else changes first.

What I learned in trauma camp helped me head into summer with new joy and new self-awareness tools. One of those was the realization that I didn't have to stay on the drama triangle at all. I could instead move toward the antidote, which is taking 100 percent responsibility.

When I first heard this idea, it sounded so nuts that I rejected it immediately. If that's you right now, I get it. But I gently invite you to hear me out and then try it on. After all, you know you've been rounding the bases on the drama triangle. Maybe you've spent enough of your life doing that.

So what is 100 percent responsibility? It means that I am 100 percent responsible for my own physical, emotional, and spiritual well-being. This means that I no longer have to wait to be happy until my son acts the way I want him to act. Instead, I am responsible for my own well-being. I choose to step into happiness, not wait for the world to get perfect around me so then I can be happy.

What is the alternative view to 100 percent responsibility? Well, normally we live as if responsibility was a pie that we divide between us. I might say to Tiffany, "You have 50 percent of the responsibility, and I have the other 50 percent." Now we enter the game of constant negotiation and a subtle shift into the drama triangle.

How? I look around the house and notice that Tiff hasn't done her share of the chores. Now, I can blame her (villain) for not doing her work, or I can step into the hero role and take more than my share of responsibility. We do this dance as the default mode in our life to such an extent that it is hard to even see that we're doing it.

But after trauma camp, as the summer is getting closer and I'm waking up to the fact that I've been in victim mode, I begin to step into 100 percent responsibility. If I don't give my son (or anyone else, for that matter) the power to take me out emotionally, then I can start to dream about what an amazing summer might be like. It is as if an amazing summer is a real possibility. I'm opening up to the reality that I can make some choices. I can exercise some agency. I can't control the extent of my son's challenges on a given day, but I can control how I respond—not just externally, but internally too. I can live into joy in the midst of the storm.

I wanted to turn this new awareness into action, so I took out a blank sheet of paper and wrote, "What would a joyful summer feel like?" across the top. What would I need to do to make this more likely? I took my dreaming to Tiff. At first, she was very nervous to even entertain the idea that the summer wasn't just going to suck. Hope was so fragile. Pro tip for any couples out there navigating this together: Go slowly and with tremendous grace.

Our initial conversation was something like:

Me: So, in the summer, all of the programs pretty much shut down for Raylan, right?

Tiff: Yes.

Me: And we still try to get work done while also juggling both kids in a nonstop entertainment/therapy rhythm, right?

Tiff: Yes.

Me: What if we didn't have to have that rhythm?

Tiff: (suspicion in voice) That would be amazing ... but we don't have any choice.

Me: What if we decided to have an incredible summer?

Tiff: (more suspicion in her voice) What would that even look like?

   (Beneath her words was the tone that said, *You might as well be telling me that I can fly if I just believe hard enough.*)

Me: What if we traveled for the summer? The world has the internet, so we could stay connected to work, and the kids love the beach. What if we just got out of here?

Tiff: But what if Raylan has a hard time?

Me: Raylan is likely going to have some challenges no matter where we are. I don't want us to shrink from challenges. Maybe we can keep growing?

At this point, Tiff brought up excellent points about all the practical matters. She is very wise that way. We worked through them. But it is important to see that we wouldn't have even gotten to practical questions if we had still believed we were stuck.

So what happened? Through a friend of a friend, we found a casita in Costa Rica that we could rent for a month. The whole month was the cost of a week in Florida. We stayed in a mud-road surf village forty-five minutes from a gas station. There were howler monkeys in the trees, and the waves were so big they could knock you down in six inches of water. We had a mango tree and an avocado tree in the yard. Penelope broke her arm on an old playground, and I learned how to say, "I need an X-ray" in Spanish (*"Yo necesito un radiografia"*). Raylan spent hours standing in the ocean with a look of incredible joy.

By far, the best part was that our family began to believe that we could do new things. There was no default future. We could actually have a new life. I began to learn how to step off the drama triangle.

Spiritually, one of the most profound things that happened for me was that I began to believe the promise of Jesus that He came to give life and give it to the full: "I came that they may have life and have it abundantly" (John 10:10b).

This is such an easy idea to dismiss or to cast so far into the future that it has no real impact on our daily experience. But the idea that Jesus, the source of all life, has now come in person to connect us *into* that life, fully and abundantly, is not an abstract concept. Here we have the source of all life—the *source*—saying, "I am here, fully in the loving embrace of My Father, inviting you into that same embrace." It is like someone telling a light bulb that has never been plugged in that it was made to connect to the electricity flow. It was meant to glow.

Jesus is inviting you to glow up.

However, almost instantly, we will have a reason (usually, many of them) that this is not possible for us right now. We have a laundry list of worries and secret shames that we think make us unworthy of this love and life, or we've bought the lie that life is suffering (see: drama triangle). So sure, we will have abundant life someday, but that day is actually after we die.

As we mentally run down our lists, we step back from the reality of this offer of abundant life, and we can feel ourselves inwardly shrinking, shoulders contracting. Even our energy levels get lower.

This is happening because we have limited our possibilities to what we can bring about on our own. We have ridden out the ups and downs of our life and said, "That is it. I can do this much, but no more. I can't do that. I can go only this far." We have, in some deep way, bought into a spiritual lie that Jesus can't change the situation. That Jesus can't expansively change our experience of life right now.

But over and over again, He breaks in and radically changes the lives of those He interacts with. In the Gospels and in our lives, we see Him heal, feed, and teach, and we see that those who encounter Him have their current (and future) experience radically expanded. The kingdom breaks in, lives are plugged into the life-giver, and lo and behold, abundant life begins to happen.

Turns out light bulbs glow when they get plugged in.

What I'm getting at here is a series of questions that each of us needs to wrestle with:

- Has my spiritual imagination flatlined?
- Have I bought the lie that my life is meant to be filled with apathetic days in which Jesus feels far off and the triune God of the Bible is not the whirlwind and fire breaking into the here and now?
- Have I made an internal decision that the living God is static and more or less done with me?

I think so many of us have made this decision, and with it, we've trained ourselves on what to expect. And it's not much. This has neurological ramifications. Neuroplasticity research is showing us that when we expect and then experience the same thing over and over again—say, spiritual apathy with a deadening of our imagination—our neural pathways take on that shape.[6] This makes it far more likely that we will continue to experience life this way.

So what should we do instead?

Fix our eyes on Jesus. There is a reason God gives us this instruction. Gaze upon Him—His full life, death, and resurrection. Meditate on His life-giving words, promises, and incredible invitation to live abundantly. Right now! Not someday. And as we meditate, imagine, sense, and feel things, our actual brains begin to change. We can experience the life abundant *now*. We can feel this expansive, joyful life breaking into ours. Our shoulders relax, our breathing gets deeper, we step more calmly into our days.

Another way to get at this same truth is to ask the question, "Did God make us to limp through life aghast at the world around us, simply waiting for death so our life can really begin?"

Think of the absurdity of that! Christians believe death has been conquered—not simply put on hold, delayed, or given a minor setback. If death has been conquered, life is what reigns now and has reigned ever since the kingdom broke in with the ministry of Jesus. Life broke into death when God Himself took on flesh and walked among us. That life was so powerful, so abundant, so lively that death didn't stand a chance. It had to die.

In that life, the ultimate life, the life of Christ, our life is hidden. In other words, our life, our very existence, our essence, is caught up with His life. This life has begun, and it has begun in fullness. "I came that they may have life and have it abundantly" (John 10:10b). These words of Jesus are true right this second for you.

But most of us hear these words of Jesus and then look back at the world around us and say, "No, what I see in the world is true. That's reality." When we do this, which by the way is our natural inclination, we are committing to live out of the reality of the world and letting that view shape us as it has always done.

There is a famous story of a horse that was tethered to a tree as a young colt. At first, it fought the rope and pulled and strained for freedom. It walked and ran in a circle, testing the limits at each side. But the rope was strong and the horse was young and weak. Over the years, the rope started to fray and rot. Eventually, it snapped. The horse was older and stronger, so it now had the ability to walk in freedom. But every day you could see it walking the same well-trod circle. Around and around, exactly at the same limits it had always known. It had defined the extent of its reality long ago and then was unable, or refused, to see a new reality.

There are those in the faith who say, "Yes, Jesus is good, and His life is in us and with us, but we are still so frail because of the fall of man and the ruining of this world. We may walk only so far because ultimately the rope will snap you back."

To this I say we have given far more credit to the power of the rope—sin and death—than we ought to have done. The life that is bursting forth in us, the very life that was at work in the risen body of Jesus Christ, is calling us to step outside that well-trodden rut and walk the path of full freedom in Christ.

It is calling us to move with His life, to love with His love, to dream of His kingdom, and to begin with all energy and joy to pray and enact the words, "Our Father in heaven, hallowed be your name. Your kingdom come, your will be done, on earth as it is in heaven" (Matt. 6:9–10).

Take up the new life. Go forth and bring a little heaven right here on earth. Leave this well-trodden path of the rope behind you. You are no longer bound.

PRACTICE: The Drama Triangle

1. Get still. Breathe.
2. Get curious. Ask, "Where in my life am I living on the drama triangle?"
3. Write it down. Name it.
4. Ask yourself, "What would it look like to take 100 percent responsibility for my physical, spiritual, and emotional well-being?"

PS: If you are tempted here to say, "I'm not responsible for my spiritual well-being—Jesus is!" there is a sense in which you are correct. However, "The old has passed away; behold, the new has come" (2 Cor. 5:17b). If you are an image bearer of the Most High God and have the Holy Spirit dwelling within you, then right now you have everything you need to move into responsibility for your spiritual growth.

He loves you. He died for you. He has given you His Spirit! Let's go!

———————

Chapter 6

Problems to Solve

Don't wish for less problems; wish for more skills.

Jim Rohn, *The Ultimate Jim Rohn Library*

The text reads, "Maybe I should just wrap my car around a tree. You and the kids would be better off." As I try to absorb the words, my heart beats both faster and slower at the same time. It feels like skipping and falling.

It is the close of the summer, and the kids are going back to school. I have never before felt two things so profoundly. On the one hand, the Lord is meeting me every day. A friend asks why I seem so lighthearted. I try to explain that over the course of my life, I have received occasional sips of living water. As if I got the smallest taste of the abiding Spirit. But I never knew exactly when or why it would happen. They were just these occasions when my soul felt afire with the love of God. But I couldn't explain it, much less hold on to it.

Now it feels as if a wellspring of life is flowing within me every day. Joy, as true and solid as the ground my feet stand on, is right there.

All the time now. I'm not sure my friend understands when I try to explain. I can tell because he changes the subject.

All this joy, and yet simultaneously there is such deep pain. Just as real and just as daily. Tiffany's depression has come back. Hence the text. Maybe it never left. I'm not sure I understand the rhythms of these things. The last time this happened, it nearly sunk me. I felt myself go into full caretaker mode. I existed only as a duty-bound automaton. Like a robot nurse who stuffs everything down just to survive. Yet the joy is still there along with the pain. I am feeling all of it.

One truth on the journey of Spirit-led self-awareness is that, as you go deeper toward self, you will feel everything more deeply. There is no way around it. Turns out there is no depth without digging.

On the one hand, this is pure exhilaration. Like being a painter who has lived only in a black-and-white world then suddenly has magenta and cerulean to work with. On the other hand, the black-and-white and shades of gray may be boring by comparison, *but* you know them. That world has the comfort of predictability, and it never asks much of you.

The journey of self-awareness means that all of you begins to come alive. You are a human in blossom.

The text Tiffany sent requires a response. What does one say to suicidal ideation? Is there an emoji for this? Perhaps a well-thought-out GIF? Mentally I find myself hiding behind humor. There is in me, at the same time, an intense sorrow and a bubble of laughter. The laughter stems from how absurdly clueless I feel in the face of this. I love her so much, and I so want to alleviate her pain. And I am staring my own limitations directly in the face.

To love someone who goes through acute depression is to love someone you know you cannot save. Tiffany's diagnosis of Complex PTSD means that the lowercase-*t* trauma of the everyday intensity of life with a child with disabilities can take her out at the knees. She begins to disassociate and withdraw. In this season, she looks to sleep as her only real escape. The weight of our daily rhythms, just the normal stuff of life—laundry, vacuuming, school drop-offs—is taking a toll. I begin to take on more and more. Work is still a lot. The needs of my son are still a lot. And now it feels like I don't have Tiff by my side.

I can go into hardcore hero mode. My whole life, I've been taught how to do work. So I roll up my sleeves. One of my mantras is, "When in doubt, do the dishes." When Raylan is dysregulated and destructive, I can feel overwhelmed just by the raw amount of cleaning and repair work in front of me every day. When I start feeling like it's too much, I notice that feeling, and I do the dishes. When I do, the feeling of overwhelm lessens just a touch, and I begin to see the pieces and not feel crushed by the whole.

My old pattern invites me back into this way of being. It tells me, "Tiff is really sad, and you should somehow make her not sad." I would then obsess about how to do the work of "un-saddening" another human. I would inevitably fail because cheering someone up for thirty seconds is very different from healing their clinical depression. Then I would move on to the next stage—resentment and anger. In terms of the drama triangle from the last chapter, I would move to the villain role and think it's all her fault.

Eventually, my old pattern would land me at utter despair and the conclusion that everything sucks now and will always suck.

But through Spirit-led self-awareness, I now know this pattern. This changes everything.

When I was a kid, I was obsessed with GI Joes. I collected them at every birthday and Christmas for years. The best part of the toys was that they had a corresponding television show. I could reenact the battles I saw on TV in the comfort of my bedroom. Amazing.

At the end of every episode, they would have this little clip of a non–GI Joe character being rescued by a "Joe" from the show. It bridged the gap between the show and my reality. This kid wouldn't be wearing black tights and a ski mask and have a kung-fu ninja grip. He would be a regular kid in a T-shirt and blue jeans. Relatable. He would inevitably be in a dangerous situation.

My favorite was the time when Snake Eyes taught a kid how to swim when it looked like he might be dragged out to sea. The show got very specific and demonstrated the scissor-kick move for treading water. At the end of these vignettes, they gave each other high fives and said, "Now you know. And knowing is half the battle."

Now I know my pattern, and knowing is half the battle, right?

Turning head knowledge into heart knowledge—and then hand knowledge—might just be the path to wisdom. This is the process of connecting what we know in our heads with the lived center of our lives (our hearts), and then taking all of that and moving toward action (hands). I knew my pattern, but how would I disrupt it? How would I feel something different and do something differently?

When I hit a brick wall, I tend to wonder what I could do differently. If you've ever seen an ant, you know that when they hit an obstacle, they just go around it. One way or another, they continue down the path they are committed to. I'm like that, and I love this about myself. It makes me loyal and disciplined.

However, it has a shadow side: I can get hyper-critical of myself. If I can't immediately overcome said brick wall, a voice comes and says something like, "Wow, you suck at this." Then I add on to that another inner voice that says, "Stop being so mean, you jerk." Now I have the aforementioned multiple inner critics.

For those of us who grew up in the church, there is another potential pitfall here: some of us believe the Holy Spirit is our inner critic. In my home church, it was a given that when you felt self-condemned, that was just the Holy Spirit reminding you oh so subtly that you are awful. However, this simply cannot be true. It is the Lord's kindness that leads us to repentance, after all (see Rom. 2:4). I assume you have experienced kindness before. It is wonderful. It feels soft, thoughtful, and full of mercy and compassion. That is kindness.

The Holy Spirit is not your inner critic.

Has anyone ever learned repentance from a voice of nonstop attack that seems to know all of our internal struggles like a psychological jujitsu master? This voice is not looking to build up but to take down. This is not kindness but accusation. The main biblical figure we know who is associated with hateful accusation is someone whose name means "accuser": Satan.

It is beyond strange, then, that so many of us have attached the identity of the Holy Spirit to the voice of our inner critic. Like we have some sort of inner David Goggins/marine drill sergeant pushing us to be our maximum-best spiritual selves. And when we see gaps, because there will be gaps, we get attacked.

In the face of Tiffany's depression, I knew old patterns. I knew my inner critics would get to work. I moved toward them with compassion. I got still. I asked the abiding Holy Spirit to be with me. I moved in empathy and self-compassion. I learned how to be present in the face of Tiff's depression and my inability to magically fix it. For a fixer, this is profoundly uncomfortable.

The result of this self-compassion was an epic shift in my way of thinking. It coalesced in the form of a fully articulated belief: *I am not a problem to solve but a person to know and enjoy.* I am not a problem. I don't need to look at myself like some sort of equation to solve, which was exactly what I was doing. Something like, "If I can fix myself, then I can apply the same fix to Tiffany, and we will all be okay." But God didn't create us as problems to solve. He created us as a blessing—He calls you "very good" (see Gen. 1:31)—and His finished work on the cross brought us back into that blessing.

Theologically, I wouldn't have said, "I am working to save myself," but I acted like the cross got me *some* of the way there, but I was still a hot mess that needed to somehow get the rest of the way there on my own. Oh, the toxicity of this belief system in me! It meant every day I viewed myself as one long difficulty to resolve. Therefore, everything in my life had to somehow serve my ability to solve this problem.

I once knew a doctor who, before attending medical school, had loved to read fiction. But once his schooling started, it was so intense and the demands so all-consuming that he read nothing but textbooks. He told me, "If it wasn't accretive to my work, then I had no time for it." I didn't know the word *accretive*. I looked it up. "Something that is growing by a series of additions."[1] In other words, if it didn't add to his medical knowledge, it was useless.

I knew what he meant. When my life was lived as a problem to solve, everything had to help solve the problem. I was the problem. But the Holy Spirit rearranged my thinking until I saw that I am not a problem to solve but a person to know and enjoy. I thought, *Wait ... I don't have to solve me? I can actually know and enjoy myself? I can step away from ever-present self-loathing that I've wrapped in theological terms and baptized with biblical language?*

Perhaps this doesn't seem like a big deal to you. I don't know what your relationship is like with your inner critic. But this felt so different that I would describe it with a feeling akin to internal spaciousness. As if I had gone from being cramped in the back of a Honda Civic hatchback to riding in a Yukon XL. I didn't know it was okay to have this much room! The God of the universe loved me so much that it began to be okay for me to love me too.

As this shift in thinking started to move from head to heart to hands, I started to exhibit more fruit of the Spirit: love, joy, peace, patience, kindness, goodness, faithfulness, gentleness, and self-control (Gal. 5:22–23a). Since there was no longer an existential bomb ticking inside me, I found it much easier to be present and still with those around me. It was very good.

The next aha moment came one morning in my contemplative prayer time. I was praying for Tiffany, asking the Lord to meet her in her depression, when I felt the Spirit move. It wasn't a voice so much as a feeling. *Tiffany is not a problem to be solved either, but a person to be known and enjoyed.* I was dumbstruck. My eyes were watering with gratitude as I knelt in prayer.

It may seem obvious to you that if *I* am not a problem to be solved, then it logically follows that Tiff can't be a problem to be solved either. But sometimes I am slow on the uptake.

Immediately, I saw that this thought applied to everyone. *You* are not a problem to be solved, but a person to be known and enjoyed. The first people I practiced this belief with were Tiffany, Raylan, and Penelope.

Old habits die hard, and so do old internal project managers. What this new belief required of me was a commitment to no longer try to "solve" my family members. This required that I commit to no longer trying to control them for a desired outcome. The outcome I was after usually took the form of, "Let me fix you based on my interpretation of how you are a problem for me right now." Now, to be utterly clear, no member of my family actually needs me to "fix" them. It was my own false internal narrative that had framed them that way.

Your family life might not be affected by disability or depression. I don't know your patterns or rhythms. But if you are in relationship with people, then perhaps you can relate to that moment when they stop being someone you are in relationship with and start becoming problems you are trying to project-manage.

Philosopher Martin Buber talked about this idea with the terms *it* and *thou*.[2] When I approach you as a *thou*, I'm genuinely honoring your humanity, even recognizing the image of God in you, your little slice of God's creativity and glory. I think of you as an equal, someone deserving of honor. But when I see you as an object, you become an *it*. A lesser thing. Something to be dealt with. To hold someone as a thou means to see them and seek to experience them as a person.

To know and enjoy someone means to get close enough to understand them. Knowledge of someone else, true knowledge, is grounded in the idea of seeking understanding. When they are a problem to solve, we don't have to understand—we just have to fix them or move them to where they need to be. It is mechanistic by definition and *not* human. To know them is to understand them.

To enjoy them is to go one step beyond understanding. It is to see enough about them and their own unique image-bearing quality to experience just a touch of delight. As if your knowledge of them leads to an organic appreciation of them. This is the enjoyment of another.

Practically, there was one thing that had to happen as a direct result of this new dawning reality: Tiff and I had to have a very hard conversation.

There is a special kind of hell you experience when you come home from work not knowing if your wife will be alive or not. If she is alive, you begin to do the laundry and maybe make the kids some mac and cheese. It is a switch from dread to the normalcy of domestic life. You hold your breath every step until you get to the bedroom to check on your loved one. On this day she is okay and I begin to breathe while I grab the hamper.

However, with this new truth (that no one is a problem to be solved), my fear was transformed. I no longer entered the home with dread but a kind of hopeful acceptance. I trusted that no matter the outcome, the Lord was with me and with Tiff. His living Spirit was alive and at work in her just as He was in me. Since I was no longer positioning her as my problem to solve, I could get focused on knowing and enjoying her.

I spot my opportunity to have the conversation one night after the kids are in bed. I sit next to Tiff and ask if we can talk. Even that was a shift. I don't demand. I don't force. I move toward her with the gentleness of an invitation.

> **Me:** Can we talk about the suicidal thoughts you've
> been having?
>
> **Tiff:** (Gives an intense stare that says something like
> *Back off.*)
>
> **Me:** (Awkwardly waits.)
>
> **Tiff:** (Shoulders drop, breathes out a held sigh of
> frustration with a tinge of relief.) Okay.
>
> **Me:** I love you and I'm not going anywhere.
>
> **Tiff:** Okay ...?
>
> **Me:** But your depression ... I think I used to think it
> was my job to fix you ... to be your caretaker. I don't
> think that's my job anymore.
>
> **Tiff:** (with heat in her voice) It was never your job. I
> just want you to be my husband.
>
> **Me:** I'm sorry I tried to take on that job for so long.
> Sounds like that was frustrating.
>
> **Tiff:** (starts to tear up) It was. I didn't ask you to take
> on that job.

> **Me:** I'm scared of your depression, and I'm scared of your suicidal thoughts.
>
> **Tiff:** (nods) I get that.
>
> **Me:** It's like I see you in your depression, and I want to somehow get in there and push you out … or build a ladder so you can climb it yourself or something. But I am starting to see that your depression, your sadness, is your work to do, not mine. I can stay here on the edge of it, I can hold space for it and be present with you, but I can't try to climb in there anymore.
>
> **Tiff:** I think I want that too. Just be with me. Don't try to be in it. It is not yours.

She begins to outline the bare bones of a plan. She will start to see a new counselor and find a psychiatrist for medication management. She is committed to taking the steps toward something else, something new. She is scared, and I understand. I am bursting with hope. We hold each other for just a second. Something sacred has happened here, and we can both feel it. We have moved a little closer toward knowing each other.

As I've mentioned, awareness works like a spotlight. Where your focused attention goes, so goes your awareness. As soon as I began to focus the spotlight on what I appreciated about Tiffany, the strangest thing happened: I started to notice more and more things I enjoyed about her.

In pop psychology, this is sometimes referred to as the yellow car phenomenon.[3] On your way to work, you don't notice any yellow cars.

Then a friend tells you they just bought one. You think it's odd because you never see them. On the way home, you notice five. What just happened? Are there suddenly more yellow cars on the road? No. You just haven't been looking for them, so they slipped right past you.

This is caused by a part of our brain called the reticular activating system (RAS).[4] It is about two inches long and the width of a pencil. It takes in all your sensory data (except for smell). It deals with so many data points that it has gotten very good at sifting through input to find the most relevant and important things to kick up to your awareness level. If it had to pay attention to all sensory input all the time, your brain would crash like a computer. The RAS helps bridge the gap between the data of the external world and your awareness.

As I looked to enjoy Tiffany more, I noticed more things that I appreciated about her. Even now, my gratitude toward her grows organically. Not in some saccharine, Hallmark-movie way that feels disingenuous but in a real way. A tender way. A kind way. In the mornings now when I wake her up, I share the latest thing I'm grateful for. She shares one with me in return.

Slowly but surely, we are moving away from viewing each other as problems to solve and are beginning to experience each other as people to be known and enjoyed.

The final aha mantra moment came a few months later.

Picture me out running one morning. Just a short jog around the neighborhood. I am listening to Maverick City Music and maybe dancing a little. Suddenly, a thought and a feeling jolt through my body from head to toe. I don't know how else to describe it besides lightning and light. What shouts across my mind is, *God is not a problem to be solved, but a person to be known and enjoyed!*

My knees go weak. I know in the deepest part of my being that this is true. This awareness is not like an intellectual exercise or a logic problem mapped out one step at a time. It arrives fully formed.

I think it is perhaps a common, or maybe even a necessary, first step to begin our journey of faith to see God as a problem to solve—or at least a mystery. As children, we ask questions like, "Where does God live?" "What does God look like?" "Did God make me?" "Did God make the dinosaurs?" "Why did He let Grandma die?" "Does she live with Him now?" "*Why* did God make me?"

These are natural questions that bubble to the surface as a child's personality comes online. They are similar to how a child might ask about a tree, an airplane, or the ocean. Kids want to understand.

My daughter asked me the other day how crayons are made. I explained to her what little I knew, and then we watched two YouTube videos that demonstrated the process. After that, she stopped asking. She had received her answer. She comfortably understood crayon origins.

Yet the very nature of God means that this is not possible to do for Him. There are no two-minute explainer videos that capture His entirety (although the Bible Project does an excellent job on this front). Each question a child asks leads to a new view of the expansive horizon. When my daughter asks what God looks like and I tell her that God is spirit and doesn't have a body (although Scripture uses physical metaphors), now we are off into a discussion of the nature of spirit.

At some point, though, I believe theological discussions can turn into a sort of intellectual angst that feels untenable. If everything else is understandable, why not God? I know for me, at least, I soon moved into problem-solving mode. *I must solve God.*

Back to my run: I suddenly understand that God is not a problem to solve, and I am now utterly free. God is a person. Three in one. A trinitarian dance of relationship. In my problem mode, the Trinity bothered me. I had to explain away this tension. The mystery of it. The abiding question mark of the abiding God was too much.

Now I laugh about it. I ask God if He has been waiting for this moment, and I feel laughter ripple through me. It reminds me of the Chronicles of Narnia, and how C. S. Lewis described what it felt like to be a child near Aslan. For the first time in a long time, I feel my childlike hand rest in the hand of my Maker. I run home laughing.

PRACTICE: Not a Problem Series

In order for you to turn these ideas into something meaningful, you have to practice them. For this practice, I invite you to go slowly. Think in terms of months, not days. Start with this morning meditation:

1. Get still. Carve out some space in a place where you can be alone.
2. Breathe.
3. When you feel settled in yourself, say, "I am not a problem to be solved but a person to be known and enjoyed." Start by saying it to yourself in your

innermost being. Then start to say it out loud. "I am not a problem to be solved but a person to be known and enjoyed."

4. Notice what comes up for you. Is there more peace? A sense of well-being? Or do you notice discomfort? Is there a friction point that you found here? Some part of you that might be resisting this shift from viewing yourself as a problem to a person? If you notice this friction, just observe it. Don't try to fix, solve, or manage it. If you'd like to do so, write it out, draw it out, or walk it out.

5. I hope this idea settles into your innermost being and clicks into place in a way that feels like, *Ahhhh, this is true.* If it does, awesome.

Now repeat this process with the second truth:

1. Get still. Some time and place where you can be alone.

2. Breathe.

3. When you feel settled in yourself, think about one or more of the other people in your life and in the world, and say, "You are not a problem to be solved but a person to be known and enjoyed." Start by saying it to yourself in your innermost being. Then start to say it out loud: "You are not a problem to be solved but a person to be known and enjoyed."

4. Notice who comes up for you. Who is the *you* that floats to the surface of your mind? Is this a person you are in conflict with? Someone you have unsettled feelings toward? Don't try to understand it all at once. Just notice that they fill the space of "problem to solve" for you.

5. Shift to curiosity. What would it look like to know and enjoy them? Is this even possible? There may be those who have abused, oppressed, or neglected you in such profound and traumatic manners that this would not be safe. Check in with your body. Are you feeling rising panic and fear? If so, this might be your body's invitation for you to do some deep work around this person. At this point, I would invite you to seek professional counseling with a practitioner who can help you unpack this in person. A book like this is a wonderful delivery method for ideas and practices, but it cannot replace the voice and physical presence of a loving counselor.

6. If this idea settles into your innermost being and clicks into place in a way that feels like, *Ahhhh ... this is true*, wonderful. You might find that you need to come back to this process repeatedly as you gain an awareness of additional people in your life whom you tend to put into the position of *problem* in your mind. Our kids are wonderful examples of

this. We love them, and they are a lot of intense work. When you notice that you are in problem mode about someone, just come back to stillness. Ask the Spirit to lead you to a place of enjoyment and tenderness toward this person.

The third truth can be one of the hardest to walk out in a meaningful way. We might be able to theologically agree that God is a person we are meant to be in a relationship with, but our lived reality might be far from this truth.

Once again, give yourself permission to be where you are.

1. Get still. Some time and place where you can be alone.
2. Breathe.
3. When you feel settled in yourself, say, "God is not a problem to be solved but a person to be known and enjoyed." Start by saying it to yourself in your innermost being. Then start to say it out loud: "God is not a problem to be solved but a person to be known and enjoyed."
4. Notice what comes up for you. Is there more peace? A sense of well-being? Or do you notice discomfort? Is there a friction point here? Some part of you that might be resisting this shift from viewing God as a problem to a person you were made to know and enjoy? If you notice this

friction, just observe it. Don't try to fix, solve, or manage it. If it feels good to do so, write it out, draw it out, or walk it out.

5. If this idea settles into your innermost being, clicks into place in a way that feels like, *Ahhhh ... this is true*, fantastic.

In all these things, remember: You are not alone. You have the Most High God dwelling in you through the power of the Holy Spirit. God loves you and will cradle you in the palm of His hand as you walk out this new way of being, gently and with kindness.

———————

Chapter 7

The Gift of Consistency

Incremental progress that is directionally correct.

Jerry Colonna, *Reboot*

We have a school event for our daughter, a meet-the-teacher evening, and Tiff and I are mapping out a strategy as if we are executing a moon landing. We have become excellent at scanning for anything that could be a hurdle, friction point, or trip wire for Raylan.

That might sound like overkill, but the amygdala of anyone who has lived in a high-intensity situation for a long time lives in an awareness state.[1] Some of this is driven by fear, and some is driven by the simple desire to make sure that Penelope is the center of attention when she meets her new teacher.

We decide to drive two cars so that if our son starts to have a hard time, I can leave with him. "Hard time" usually means that he has experienced a sensory overload. We know this is happening when he starts to go nonverbal, heads for an exit with no warning, or starts to stim more than usual. All of these are ways he tries to self-regulate. We want to be clued in to these moments to better support him.

"Hard time" could also be the result of something happening socially that he doesn't understand. Social confusion is becoming a bigger and bigger deal for him, and we have not yet figured out how to explain the ins and outs of preteen behavior to our sweet boy. His social confusion often escalates to dysregulation (a.k.a. anger and frustration so huge that he loses control of his body ... and things start to break).

We have 467 flavors of "hard time" in our house that we are constantly trying to pre-defuse. It's as if we live in a suspense movie where we are always asking, "Which wire do I cut ... the blue or the red?"

As we enter the school, we hear the noise and see the bottleneck of parents and kids at the double doors. Tiff and I look at each other. It is the look that says, *This is not ideal*. It is often followed by the look that says, *Should we already bail on this as too much?* I move my eyebrows in that magic marriage communication that indicates she should go on with Penelope and I will stay with Raylan. Tiff understands instantly. As they move off down the hallway, I check in with Raylan. He wants to go back outside.

Out in the spaciousness of the front lawn, he begins to calm down. I can see it in his shoulders. He sees some friends he used to play flag football with and runs off to play. I am thankful again for how much he loves being with other kids. Other parents with kids on the autism spectrum have told me about how hard it is to socially connect them to peers. No issues here. I see a huge smile break out on Raylan's face as he jumps into the game of football that is organically emerging on the lawn.

I sit on a bench and try to get still again. As I've gone on with the journey of self-awareness, I've noticed that my healthy habits aren't limited to my morning rhythms or nighttime prayers. Contemplation has spilled out into every moment of my day, almost in a pray-without-ceasing manner. I have begun to get a taste of that elusive idea of Paul's. Moments before, when it was clear that Raylan was not going to make it through that noisy hallway, I had tensed up. I felt it in my body as a strumming vibration, like a drawn bow with an arrow nocked. It was anxiety.

There have been so many moments when we didn't know his limits. When we tried to force or push him into something that was clearly not for him. When you start out as a new parent, you just don't know yet what you need to know to do the job well. God save all of our firstborns. However, with typically developing children, you start to get discernible feedback: I like this; I don't like this.

Remember that frustration when you had an infant crying in your arms and you tried everything to soothe them? You fed them, you changed them, you rocked, you stood up, you sat down, you paced, you changed them again because ... *please help me, I don't know what to do because I don't know what you want!* This is what it has been like to be the dad of this amazing kid. I want to know his interior world, and I have such a limited view.

Early on, we pushed, cajoled, begged, and pleaded. And he melted down. The reality was that he was telling us everything we needed to know. He was communicating. But we were blind to it at first. We kept waiting to get the information from him in ways we expected.

I remember one moment when we were visiting a wonderful church that had a special needs ministry. It was in a nice part of town where zero cars had scratches or dents. I was careful as we parked. There was a maze of classrooms we had to navigate to reach the childcare area, where we would meet the one-on-one "buddy" who was going to help Raylan stay engaged with Sunday school. We were so grateful to be there, and Tiff and I were so tired that it began to mean a lot to us to get him checked in as quickly as possible.

The hallway was too loud, the check-in booth too far away from the door, and the other kids too chaotic as they streamed around us. Raylan lost it. He threw himself on the floor and began to scream at the top of his lungs. His whole body thrashed, and he kicked over a few five-foot-high displays advertising the latest Bible study series for parents to grow closer to God and their kids. Those Bible studies looked so good.

Tiff got on the floor with him, trying her best to soothe him to bring him back into himself. I stood there frozen. I remember a deep sense of shame and a gaping mouth of fear that seemed like it just might swallow me. If you have never been the parent of the kid who looks for all the world to just be throwing a tantrum while some other kid strolls by like the popular teen in an eighties movie (complete with sweater tied around neck*), then you may find this hard to relate to. You are simultaneously the worst parent in the world *and* the one who most needs the parenting class on the display that your son just drop-kicked across the room. And everyone knows it.

It makes sense why I felt so tense at Penelope's meet-the-teacher event: I was afraid of that happening again.

---

*   Google "Stan Gable, *Revenge of the Nerds*."

Sitting there on the bench outside her school, all of this flashes through my mind. I've been here before. I remind myself that I am okay. That Raylan is okay. I take a long, steady breath in, another one out. I bring myself back to the present. I am grateful that the Lord, in His mercy, has given me this gift of Spirit-led self-awareness. In this moment, on this bench in front of my daughter's school, I feel gratitude well up. In my heart of hearts, I praise the Lord. I am okay. He has me right now.

One of the biggest benefits of Spirit-led self-awareness is that the more we walk this path, the more we bring it with us everywhere we go. This happens only if we give ourselves the gift of consistency. So often, the spiritual life is framed in terms of discipline, duty, or rules. As if we can turn the mystical walk with the risen Lord Jesus, who mysteriously conquered death for all humanity, into a mere checklist.

The problem is that as soon as we have framed life with the life-giver as a discipline or a duty, it begins to *feel* like a discipline or a duty. That is to say, it feels like something we *have* to do, not something we *get* to do. If we put it in that category, we will start to have a faith experience marked by fits and starts, not consistency. Like a bad New Year's resolution diet.

Have you ever been in a small group where someone says, "I know I need to be reading my Bible more and praying and stuff, but I just can't seem to get into it"? They hang their head in shame, and everyone echoes similar frustrations. Someone suggests listening to the latest sermon podcast that talks about it, and everyone promises to listen and "hold each other accountable." It is as if we have all decided we must eat more brussels sprouts. Deep down, we know we aren't going to do it, but maybe if our collective shame rises high enough, we might see some improvement.

How do we change? How do we break this pattern? How do we move from fits and starts to consistency?

What we believe about something shapes our emotional experience. If I'm driving in downtown Nashville traffic—which has become notoriously bad in recent years—and I get cut off, what I believe about what just happened affects my emotional reaction. If the story I believe is "This person is a selfish punk who only cares about themself," I will feel anger and resentment. If I believe "This person must be in an emergency situation to be driving like that," then I am moved toward empathy and might even pray they get there safely.

Now, you might be like me and *never* give a fellow driver the benefit of the doubt ... and struggle with resentment anytime you see bad behavior in traffic. I mean, they can't all be on the way to the hospital, right? But do you want to live this way? Do I? What benefit is this bringing to your life?

Our beliefs affect our emotions, which in turn affect our actions. If I think someone is a jerk for cutting me off, I'm more likely to drive aggressively in response. As if me honking and riding their bumper is going to get them to have some sort of personal breakthrough. "You know ... he's right. I do need to change how I drive. Thank you for honking so many times." If I think they are in an emergency, on the other hand, I pray. Different beliefs lead to different emotions, which lead to different actions.

This idea that our beliefs affect our emotions and our emotions in turn affect our actions is called the *cognitive triangle*. (I'm not sure why psychology uses so many triangles, but here we are.) First developed in the 1960s by Aaron Beck to be used in cognitive behavioral therapy (CBT),[2] it has helped people get a handle on their internal world. So how does it apply to shifting our devotional time with the Lord?

If we believe something is a duty or a discipline, we feel obligated. That is to say, we feel we are being forced to do something that is not fun or enjoyable. This in turn creates the emotion of low-intensity anxiety, annoyance, boredom, or dread. This can happen even with something that is meant to be delightful.

Think about it: We are—at least on paper—supposed to be the people who love being around our Maker in such a profound way that we are excited about heaven and about one day being around Him all the time in total rest and joy! But right now, we act as if spending time with Jesus is like having to hang out with that guy who goes to your church but you have nothing in common with and you're not sure why your spouse keeps saying you really should hang out with him more. What would you even talk about?

We must experience a shift in our thinking in order to give ourselves the gift of consistency. I think the answer is playful exploration.

By "playful exploration," I mean a shift in our belief about what is meant to happen in our time of prayer, meditation, and reflection. This shift needs to happen regarding both our inner world and God's ability to meet us there. If we believe that the God of heaven and earth has given us the Spirit of life, the very Spirit who raised Christ from the dead, that is a wonderful first step. We must also believe that this Spirit is whispering love to us in our innermost selves at all times. How do we know this? Scripture tells us again and again that we are a delight to the Lord and that He is our Good Shepherd who lovingly brings us back to the fold.†

This is not what I learned growing up. I was taught in Sunday school that Jesus was a good shepherd but that the shepherd would break the leg of the wandering sheep and then bring it back to the fold. This was supposedly to keep it from wandering away again, and by the time the leg healed, it would have learned to stay with the flock. However, there is no historical evidence of any good shepherd ever doing this intentionally.

Anyway, think about it for a second. How does this line up with the image of God as our shepherd from Psalm 23? At no point does it say, "Yea, though I walk through the valley of the shadow of death, I will fear no evil, because if I get too lost, God will break my leg." What? No! He will gently lead me, He will comfort me with His presence, not cause a traumatic injury that will distance us relationally.

I looked into this story, by the way. As far as I can tell, this non-biblical data point seems to have come from a 1955 book titled *What Jesus Says*, by Robert Boyd Munger.[3] Munger was apparently an amazing man who loved his wife and kids deeply, traveled the world teaching about the beauty of Christ, and pastored in California for decades. I say that to make it clear that I don't think this one illustration needs to distort a person's whole legacy. But I do think he

---

†   See Psalms 23; 36:7; 149:4; Zephaniah 3:17; Luke 15:5; John 10:11, 14; and 1 John 4:19, for examples.

got this point wrong. When you turn inward and spend more time dwelling with the Spirit, you don't find a threat; you find abiding love.

If I believe that I have the Spirit who is speaking unending love to me, then carving out time to sit in stillness with the Spirit of God is no longer threatening.

Now grounded in this love, we begin to shift toward playful exploration. What do I mean? Have you ever seen that dad at Disney World who clearly has a mental checklist about how many rides the family will do and where and when they will eat and perhaps (if there's time) use the bathroom? Have you seen the line of wilting kids following him? He somehow made Disney World joyless. To move from discipline to delight, we have to recapture the feeling of a child at play. It is with a skip and a hop, not a forced march, that the Lord invites us to know Him and ourselves. This is a joyful adventure!

One way I have found to reconnect to this part of myself that intuitively knows how to play is … to play! Is there something you currently enjoy doing so much that even thinking about it puts a smile on your face? If your answer is no, think back to a time in childhood when you engaged in lighthearted play. Don't overthink it. What comes to mind?

Get still; feel what this feels like in your body. For me it is a lightness, a bit of a tingle in my spine. It is like the edge of excitement. Ground yourself in this feeling. Invite the Spirit to lead you with this kind of openhandedness in your quiet time. Try to stay in this mental and emotional space of easy expectation. If you lose it quickly, no big deal. Try it again. Don't try to manage this or turn it into a task. As soon as that happens, we are back into checklist mode and are no longer playing.

For some of us, this might be extremely challenging. Our childhoods could have been cut short for any number of complicated reasons. If you find yourself hitting a brick wall, get curious. Ask, "Why is this so hard? What is coming up for me?" Journal it out, walk it out, or talk it out with someone who can hold nonjudgmental space with you.

When you are able to spend more time in joyful communion with the Spirit, your actions begin to change organically. You desire it more. When I first began to practice contemplative prayer, it was a five-minute discipline. Now it is a breezy hour of laughter and joy. Not through effort or willpower, like I'm on some sort of spiritual SEAL Team Six, but like the kid who rides roller coasters all day and is somehow still full of energy when the fireworks go off at the end of the day at Magic Kingdom.

This joy will, over time, lead to the gift of consistency. Consistency in turn bears fruit in every part of life.

It's time to drive home after the meet-the-teacher event, so I walk over to give Raylan a heads-up. "Five minutes and we need to leave." He asks for ten. "Sure thing." I sit in the light of the setting sun and enjoy the moment. After ten minutes, I walk over to collect him. He is upset to leave these friends but starts walking back with me. I see that he is struggling, becoming nonverbal. I'm thankful that Tiff and I drove separately. She and Penelope can ride home in peace and talk about how excited Penelope is about the upcoming school year.

As Raylan sits in the front seat next to me, he kicks off his shoes and starts to stim. He can't seem to control his body, and I can see he is so uncomfortable. I roll his window down, since sometimes the wind feels good on his face. He loves high-intensity sensory experiences if he feels he can control them. He rolls the window up and down a few times, trying to dial in the best wind angle. I'm now driving down the highway for the two miles between school and our house.

Raylan's body begins to thrash in a way that isn't safe in a moving vehicle. I'm about to pull over when I hear a loud *crack*. I glance over while trying to focus on the road and see a spiderweb pattern of glass spreading from his side of the windshield over to mine. He kicked it that hard. He didn't do it on purpose. He is still now. In shock.

Part of me instantly fills with anger and fear. My knuckles go white on the steering wheel.

But a millisecond later, I'm fully aware of all this. Hours spent sitting in that chair every morning praying, connecting with self, and meditating on the Lord's love have cultivated interior space. I am able to recognize the big feelings and welcome them while also not giving them center stage. I do not shift into Hulk mode. I remain Bruce Banner. I breathe. I look at Raylan, and I see a scared kid who doesn't know what to do with his body when he feels so many things he can't process.

"Raylan," I say, "you broke the windshield."

He nods. The glass is still held in the frame, so we can make it home safely. I get very still and calm. He responds to my calm as if it's contagious. He begins to breathe.

When we get home, Raylan heads right to his peace corner, a low-sensory area of our house where he can tune everything out. Remember what it was like to hide under a blanket as a kid and just feel safe? Like you had your own little pocket of total protection? Raylan goes to that space, and it is beautiful. It's where he can come back to himself fully.

After I get him settled, I head to the kitchen out of his line of sight. I connect with my anger and feel it fully. It washes over me like a wave. (More on this in the next chapter.) I don't shame myself for being angry; I don't hide or stuff or repress. It simply passes through, and then it is gone.

I make dinner for the kids. I turn on some music, an old favorite from the band Roman Candle. I thank the Lord that He is with me even now. That He is leading me closer and closer to Him.

That night before bed, I take time to sit in my prayer chair. I don't call it that often, but it rhymes and sounds pretty holy. I settle in and think through the moments of the day. The Lord brings to mind the distance we have covered in the last year. Twelve months before, I could not have stayed calm in the face of a cracking windshield at 65 mph, and I definitely could not have so quickly shifted back to joy. I would have freaked out, escalating the situation. Raylan would have responded with even more intensity, and it's possible that one or both of us would've been hurt in the process.

As I remember the events of the afternoon, there is none of that self-aggrandizing pride I often used to have. That "I am so awesome, and people should know I am awesome" swagger. But there is pride of another sort. It is the pride of a child of God who looks at his heavenly Father and says, "Can you believe we just did that? Aren't You proud of me? I'm learning what You are teaching me, Dad! Thanks for loving me so much and teaching me so patiently." No joke: Right there in the bedroom, I stand up and let out a "Woo-hoo!" and pump my fist.

Right as Tiff walks in and looks at me like I've finally lost it.

PRACTICE: Play

I described this practice above. Now it's your turn. Get your paper and pencil and go to your quiet place.

1. Ask yourself this question: "Is there something I currently enjoy doing so much that even thinking about it puts a smile on my face?" Write it down. (If your answer is no, think back to a time in childhood that you engaged in lighthearted play. Don't overthink it. What comes to mind? Write it down.)

2. Get still, feel what play feels like in your body. We tend to think that memory is just something in the mind, but it is not. It is a whole-body experience! For me, play feels like a lightness, with a little bit of a tingle in my spine. It is like the edge of excitement.

3. Ground yourself in whatever you are feeling. Invite the Spirit to lead you with this kind of open-handedness in your quiet time. Try to stay in this

mental and emotional space of easy expectation. If you lose it quickly, no big deal. Try it again. Don't try to manage this or turn it into a task. As soon as that happens, we are back into checklist mode and no longer playing. If it helps, remember the story of Jesus welcoming the playful children who had been denied by the overly serious disciples. Mirth is a wonderful part of the spiritual life.

———————

Chapter 8

Emotions—WTH?

We must lay before Him what is in us,

not what ought to be in us.

C. S. Lewis, *Letters to Malcolm: Chiefly on Prayer*

It is one year after trauma camp, and we are sitting in an IEP meeting at Raylan's school. Suddenly, my left eye starts to twitch. All on its own. I am not telling my left eye, *Hey, you should twitch right now in a fast-paced way that freaks out the nice vice principal sitting across from you*. But there it goes, twitching away as if it can now make independent choices.

IEP stands for "individual education plan." It's a game plan for teachers and support staff of children with a disability or diagnosis who may qualify to receive a variety of accommodations for equitable access according to their needs.

I'm very grateful for Raylan's IEP and all the staff, but these meetings are the worst.

Imagine going to the DMV while trying to learn quantum physics ... in Russian. Throw in some kind of weird poker game where the loser is your kid's education, and you kind of have a sense for these meetings. It feels this way even though I know everyone here is doing the absolute best they can.

There are six of us in the room, including the aforementioned kindhearted vice principal. Really, she is great. But right now, she is telling me what they can and can't do for Raylan according to his qualifications. And what I can't do is get past that list of "can'ts."

The way the IEP process works is that you, the parent, probably without a PhD in disability education or a master's from Harvard in early childhood development, are expected to ask the right sort of questions in such a way that your child gets all the available resources. It would be as if you are at the doctor and they are describing all the different possible procedures you could choose to keep your heart beating. But you aren't a doctor. And for most of us parents, we just don't know how to properly navigate this moment.

Tiff is sitting next to me with a binder that looks like a 1970s New York phone book. She is rapidly turning to page eighty-nine, which has a yellow tab. The page is about Raylan's reading levels, and she is trying to demonstrate that his levels have not increased high enough. She is making the case that he should get more assistance.

The educators in the room gently explain that he *is* progressing, even if it doesn't seem like enough. Meanwhile, we are seeing our sweet son get left further and further behind his peers. He is now angry and anxious about school every morning. It is a battle to get him into the car, a battle we are losing. Can't they please do something?

Hence my eye, and its independent choice to begin twitching.

These teachers love him. I can feel that in the room. There is no one throwing Raylan under the bus as if he were the problem. They are all trying to step into his world and teach him there. They are all trying to learn how he learns so they can walk with him. I love them for this. And I am also so angry and scared because there is a collective sense that we just can't do enough for this incredible kid.

Tiff and I leave this meeting feeling haggard. We are simultaneously refusing to quit the fight *and* unsure of next steps. In the coming days, Tiff decides to become certified through the Vanderbilt Volunteer Advocacy Project. I decide to try to get Raylan into one of the best schools for kids with disabilities in the Southeast. A swing for the fences.

The first major hurdle is finances. That well-resourced school is about $40,000 per year. That is not a typo. Fortunately, I have some very generous friends who have always loved Raylan and want the best for him. I call this couple and ask them if they would support this. They are in! I am constantly reminded that God sends resources to the saints so that saints can bless those around them. And we are being abundantly blessed by the generosity of our community.

Next, we go through the intense application process. This takes about six weeks and includes a multi-hour evaluation of Raylan that we pay for out of pocket. So far, so good. We are making headway, and I see a little light at the end of the tunnel.

Then the admissions director calls me to set up the full campus tour. At least, that is what I think the call is about. It goes like this:

Admissions Director (AD): So, Mr. Acuff, thank you for taking the time to go through our whole process.

Me: You're welcome. We're just really excited for him to get the help he needs.

AD: (awkward pause) Well ... you see ... it's just that we don't think Raylan would be a good fit here.

Me: (shocked silence)

AD: Mr. Acuff?

Me: Why?

AD: Well, you see, his level of autism is more than we can accommodate in our normal programming.

Me: What do you mean?

AD: We don't think he would do well here.

Me: What do you mean?

AD: Kids with the severity and intensity of the challenges your son shows ... Well, we are just not set up in a way to serve them well.

Me: Ma'am, aren't you the best school in the area for students with disabilities?

AD: Yes, we are.

Me: (voice rising in mild panic) So surely you could figure out a way to help our son.

AD: I understand your frustration, but we cannot accommodate his needs in the classroom.

Me: (utterly incredulous at this point) So wait ... you are the best in the state and you can't help him? Where are we supposed to go?

AD: I hate to say this, but sometimes kids like your son just fall through the cracks.

I'm not sure how we got off the phone. In my head, I time-traveled to the mid-nineties, picked up the phone from the wall of my parents' kitchen, and slammed it down.

I grew up a pastor's kid in what comedian Nate Bargatze calls the "most Christian" decades of the eighties and nineties.[1] That meant, at least for me, that I learned about emotions with no small amount of shame. I'm not sure how much was overt or intended, but it was there, nonetheless. I was taught that emotions were things that happened but were not important. They were not meant to play a part in our decision-making process or our faith.

In Sunday school, we had this nice little illustration of a train with three cars: the engine (faith), the middle car (facts), and the caboose (feelings). I was taught that feelings were so unimportant that we could simply drop the caboose whenever we needed to. Got feelings you don't understand or care for? Just drop that caboose and keep rolling. You're good, right?

I was taught that feelings are not something we can fully understand, get a handle on, or base anything on. Unreliable data points. So, instead of seeking wisdom and knowledge about our feelings, we should drop the caboose. At one point, I was even taught that we should just drop the caboose in advance, since the caboose was the most likely train car to pull us into sin.

As a kid who was mildly into Thomas the Tank Engine, this all sounded a bit suspicious, but I rolled with it. The outcome? For most of my life, I believed that emotions are things we don't understand or control and that *no one on the planet* understands or controls. So you should be suspicious of them. Therefore, cultivate distrust of "emotionality" within yourself, and intentionally ignore whatever feelings may arise.

It is just too dark and confusing in there.

This was a form of evangelical stoicism that was more in line with Epictetus than it was with the fully fleshed-out characters I saw jumping off the pages of the Bible.[2] The Psalms drip with emotions; they drip with humanity. Can you imagine someone telling David, "So it turns out that most of what you are writing here is not important, even distracting, and could potentially be sinful"?

Lest you think I'm overstating the case, a recent Google search of the train illustration found this statement from a prominent Christian ministry: "You should never depend on feelings or seek after an emotional experience. The very act of looking for an emotional experience is a denial of the concept of faith, *and whatever is not of faith is sin*"[3] (italics added).

The irony here is that if you are a Christian going to church in America, you're going there seeking, at least in part, an emotional experience. It is that taste of wonder and happiness that comes when you belt out your favorite song as the band really leans into the chorus. Have you ever tried to sing a Maverick City Music song while *not* seeking an emotion? What would you even do with your hands?

As a kid, it never occurred to me to ask where emotions came from. They were presented as these mysterious entities that could make us act like we didn't want to act (à la Paul in Romans 7:14–25). Then, when I became a teenager, I was taught that emotions were lumped together with puberty and hormones. At youth group on Sunday nights, emotions were presented as the vague bad guys that we suddenly had a lot more of but that would one day pass and we could go back to normal. Thank God.

So where *do* emotions come from?

From God. He made us. And He made us as emotional beings. It is part of who we are. Not a part meant to be shamed into the shadows or suppressed with Stoic maxims wrapped in Christian logic or Bible-ese. We humans are complicated beings, and emotions are one piece of that complexity.

But if you had a car that was making a weird sound, and you found out the problem was the catalytic converter, you wouldn't throw your hands up and go, "Ugh ... that is the most mysterious part of the car. No one understands it. I guess I will simply ignore it forever and just drive with that sound."

Perhaps all this "emotions are a part of us" language is feeling too vague or squishy for you. So let me say it in the language of neuroscience:

> Emotions arise from activations of specialized neuronal populations in several parts of the cerebral cortex, notably the anterior cingulate, insula, ventromedial prefrontal, and subcortical structures, such as the amygdala, [etc.].[4]

In other words, God made us with brains. Brains are these astounding chemical and electrical systems that generate many wonderful things, including what we experience as emotions. We must get rid of this old-school idea that rational thought is good because it comes from the brain but emotions are bad because they don't. Especially since it turns out that they do also happen to come from the brain.

At a core level, emotions are simply "energy in motion."[5] Literally, energy moving through our body. So why all the panic around emotions?

I have to think that this suppression of emotions and the inherent mistrust of feelings came from a fear of, well ... how they make us feel. As if we are out of control. As if we might do something we wouldn't approve of or appreciate or feel like was honoring God. So, instead of taking the time to get curious and *know* our emotions and understand ourselves at a deep level, it was far easier to simply say "drop that whole caboose."

In the past few years, many Christian authors have been highlighting the importance of emotions in our daily existence. The neuroscientist Dr. Curt Thompson says that emotions are so critical they "could be considered to be the gasoline in our human tank. If we were to take emotion out of the human experience, we would literally stop moving."[6] This from a man who is deeply steeped in his Christian walk and considers emotional awareness to be a critical part of the life of the believer.

Pete Scazzero, author of the immensely popular series *Emotionally Healthy Spirituality*, says boldly that understanding emotions in the context of Christian faith "has led us [his church] to frontiers of life in the Holy Spirit that we could not have imagined."[7]

So if emotions are not these things that lead directly to sin, or so mysterious that we can never hope to understand them, what do we actually do with them?

When I get off the phone with the admissions director, I'm flooded with emotion. I walk out the front door of our house and just slump onto the steps. Happily, my newfound Spirit-led self-awareness now bears a little fruit. I know that I am awash in anger, fear, and sadness. In the past, I wouldn't have been able to articulate what I was feeling. And I would have minimized or hidden those emotions. I would have tried to move into action as quickly as possible. Make a new plan. Just keep going.

But I am flooded, and I know it.

There is an interesting thing about floods. Sometimes the best harvest years come right after a flood. When the water recedes, it leaves behind all sorts of nutrients. Prior to that flood, the soil may have been depleted, leached of the micronutrients it needed. But all this good stuff was sitting upstream or on the bottom of the river. The flood brings it to where it can be put to use in a new and generative way. I have found this to be true of human experience, as well.

As I sit on the front porch, breathing deeply, I name what I am feeling. I am experiencing anger. I am experiencing fear. I am experiencing sorrow. I am flooded. There is a part of me programmed to believe that feeling these things is shameful. I notice that negative message as it swims to the surface, and I gently release it. I allow myself to fully feel what I am feeling.

As this happens, I feel my body starting to relax. My fists of anger become open palms willing to receive. My chest, tight with fear, slowly becomes a place of new breath and hope. The hollow aching behind my eyes releases, and I begin to look up.

In the end, I'm able to wonder what I am about to learn. What harvest will come after this flood?

Our feelings can teach us incredible things—about ourselves, about how God made us, and about what hidden stories we might be believing under the surface. Anger, for instance, is often teaching us about a boundary we hold, either on purpose or subconsciously. Sorrow and sadness can teach us that there is a loss in our lives, maybe even one we haven't admitted to ourselves. Fear can warn us of an impending threat, real or imagined, to our physical or psychological safety.

As I sit on the steps after that disappointing phone call, I have so many incredible things to learn. My anger teaches me that I am a fierce protector of my beloved child. It is okay for me to pursue the best outcomes for him.

The false story I am believing is that this admissions director took away my only pathway to protect my son and prepare him for success. I believed she had stolen something vital from Raylan and had therefore crossed a critical boundary I was holding. As I sat with this story, I moved into curiosity: Was this actually true? Were there no other pathways to learning for Raylan in the world? Of course there were!

When I framed it in that way, I saw that it was absurd. I even chuckled just a little bit. There would be other options to explore, the admissions director was a well-intentioned person who had told me true things I needed to learn, and with the power of the abiding Spirit leading me on, I could handle whatever came next.

The deep fear I felt came from the thought that we had at long last fallen off the cliff into the unknown abyss below. If you are the parent of a kid with a disability, perhaps you know this cliff too. It is the place you find yourself when you are beyond the well-lit walkway of typical parenting.

In your frightened imagination, you believe that what you're giving up for your child is the typical K–12 education, a shot at college, and any hope of a pursuit of the American dream. It is a vision full of invitations to birthday parties and sleepovers, Little League games, and that first school dance. It is upwardly mobile and has all the best stuff.

It is most decidedly *not* full of hospital visits, overnight stays, an honorary medical degree from "YouTube University," afternoons when your kid wants to play with other kids but there are no friends anymore and you don't remember quite when the invites stopped.

It was dawning on me that we were off the path that so many parents desire for their child. That was true. The lie my fear was telling me was that this new path would be all awful all the time. That there would be only loneliness for Raylan and never a single opportunity for him to have joy again in his life. Isn't this what fear does?

In the past, I would have shamed myself for having that fear. Or perhaps I would've tried to defeat my fear or argue my fear back down into the shadows. Instead, I simply noticed it, welcomed it as a teacher, learned from it, and released it. That day on the steps, my fear taught me that I was committed to some stories that no longer served me. I began to wonder what new stories of creativity and hope about Raylan and our future I might begin to live into.

My sorrow ran deeper than the anger and fear. Oh, how uncomfortable it is to sit with our sadness and just let it have space. At this point, I went into the house to grab a notebook. I wanted to map out the path of my sorrow. I began with this statement: "I am experiencing sadness. This sadness feels connected to an imagined future where my son has no hope. I don't want my son to ever feel hopeless. Right now, I feel hopeless for my son."

In the midst of this, I invited the Spirit to be with me. I felt the nudge of the Spirit through the words of Scripture: "I will never leave you nor forsake you" (Heb. 13:5b) and "Peace I leave with you; my peace I give to you. Not as the world gives do I give to you" (John 14:27a).

I breathed into the trust of this reality. I let it settle into my bones where all real truth lives. An awareness emerged that my sorrow was directly connected to my deep love *for Raylan*, and this shifted me into gratitude. Slowly, peacefully, and without any sense of force, "I am experiencing sorrow" became "I am experiencing gratitude."

I sat there overcome with a beautiful gratitude at the reality that I get to be this kid's dad. I get to be the one fighting for him, advocating for him, making a way for him in the world in a way that feels aligned with who he is and *not* who he will never be. He is not typically developing, and that is okay. He is still fearfully and wonderfully made. What a gift Raylan is to me. What a gift Tiffany is to our family. What a fierce fellow fighter. What a gift our laughing, playful, jump-off-of-every-high-thing-she-can-find, adventure-prone daughter is to our family.

My chest is bursting with joy. It is a steady thing. A grounded-on-the-Rock kind of thing. A glowing thing that radiates an inner light generated by no one short of the Creator, who hung every star in the sky and told it how bright to be on every single night.

If you had walked past me at that moment, you would have seen a man with tears falling in a steady stream while smiling with every muscle in his face.

PRACTICE: Learning from Emotions

So what actually happened there? The first step toward what we might think of as Spirit-led emotional intelligence is that we have to be able to name our feelings. This can get daunting if we try to learn a thousand shades of feelings, like the crayon box that has rows and rows of stadium seating. I have found it helpful to use the primary colors analogy that I first read in the book *The 15 Commitments of Conscious Leadership* by Jim Dethmer, Diana Chapman, and Kaley Warner Klemp.[8]

Go with basics like blue, green, and red. We will use these to correspond with what are sometimes called our core emotions. There are a lot of different ideas out there about what our core emotions are. But whether you go with Chip Dodd's list of eight[9] or Robert Plutchik's slightly different but also insightful list,[10] the goal at this stage is to simply have the names and basic understanding.

Personally, I go with these five in my daily practice:

Anger: red

Fear: gray

Sadness: blue

Joy: yellow

Hope: green

It feels a little like Pixar's *Inside Out*, doesn't it? You might wonder, "What about anxiety?" Well, that is just fear with the volume turned down, and fear is already on the list. How about rage? That is just fully saturated anger. Sorrow? Sadness at full blast. Anticipation? Low-intensity hope.

The goal here is not a complete catalogue of all our feelings and their relatives. Nor are we trying to turn the naming of our emotions into one more thing we can manage and get absolutely right. If you feel yourself heading in that direction, take a breath, release your shoulders, and open your hands. Step into this with a spirit of play and exploration.

Once you have named what you are feeling, can you simply allow yourself to be here? Or are you noticing a sense of shame or self-condemnation for experiencing this feeling? Whatever your answer, see if you can simply allow it to be. For instance, if you are shaming yourself for feeling sadness, get curious about it and ask something like, "What story do I believe about sadness?" or "I wonder if I think sadness is a weakness?" or "Do I believe sadness is a sign of a lack of faith on my part?" Just see what comes up.

At this point, it might be helpful to walk it out or write it out. Simply take a few minutes to walk around the block and change your physical perspective. Or take a few minutes to write down your inner experience to see it in a new light.

When you are able to allow space for whatever you are feeling, it's time to shift toward a learning posture with the question, "What

Is this feeling trying to teach me right now?" If you're feeling anger, maybe frame the question like, "Is there a boundary that has been crossed in my life? Did I know that was a boundary I held? Do I still want to hold that boundary?"

Again, the goal here is not to try to ask the perfect question, as if we are suddenly FBI investigators getting to the bottom of a case. If you feel that energy, simply notice and let it go. Stay open. Stay curious. Stay kind to yourself. And stay present to the work of the Spirit.

Frequently in these moments, I will invite the Holy Spirit into the process. I know theologically that the Spirit is always with me, but I have found it helpful to intentionally make room for the work of the Spirit through a gentle invitation. For me, this is an act of faith and delightful submission. I am not alone. I am never alone. The Lord is with me even now, even here.

I end these times of deep learning by capturing on paper some of what I have learned. Sometimes I create a bullet list of ideas and thoughts. Sometimes, stream-of-consciousness paragraphs. Sometimes I jot my thoughts in the margins of my journaling Bible. The goal here is to record on the page what has transpired largely in our innermost self. There is something magical and tangible about this process, and it helps me take the lessons I've learned and build upon them.

However, let me say as clearly as possible that only you will know what feels best for you. Listen to yourself. Experiment, play, try out new paths of creativity. You might hate writing but love to paint. Amazing. You might hate painting but love taking pictures. Whatever it is that you do to capture the learnings and move forward, find your way toward it with joy.

And if at this moment you find yourself veering toward the cynical feeling of *What is the use of all this stuff?* remember that God didn't just make things useful; He also made them beautiful. Flowers didn't have to come in a million colors, but they do.

———————

Chapter 9

Alignment

A man may seem to be silent, but if his heart is condemning others he is babbling ceaselessly.

Abba Poemen, in *The Sayings of the Desert Fathers*

It is my birthday, and I'm just finishing making a giant pot of coffee. Usually, I stick to the single Keurig K-Cup maker I put near my bed for my daily practice, but today I'm expecting a crowd. One of the ways I've been staying dialed into myself is by running. Not your typical, fast-paced, I'm-trying-to-get-in-shape sort of running. But slow, measured running where my heart can stay in something called Zone 2. Zone 1 is you just sitting there not doing anything active. Zone 2 is running so slowly that you can still have a normal conversation. I like to do this kind of running for an hour or so. I think of it as long-form physical meditation.

But today I'm running with a crowd. I invited as many friends as could make it to join me for the first-ever Front Porch 50K Friendship Run. I will start at my front door and run for fifty kilometers (just over thirty-one miles). At my speed, this is an all-day kind of affair. Anyone can join, but no one knows the route but me. Today is not about speed or competition—it is about being together. Hence the mystery route. No one runs ahead. I am aiming for heart connection time. I didn't make a spreadsheet or force people to sign up for time slots. I simply said, "Text me when you can make it, and I'll tell you where I am."

This morning, there are six of us who start the run. Most go a mile or two. A few go six. Later, one friend whom I haven't seen in years runs a half marathon with me. We move at an easy pace. Sometimes talking, sometimes praying. Sometimes just listening to sounds of the greenway trail we're running on or watching birds and deer napping in the underbrush around us. The beauty of the day is that I don't run alone. Every time I'm down to just one friend, another shows up. I feel the Lord's kindness in this.

I keep thinking, *This is so much fun. I am living the exact life I want to be living.*

What I'm feeling today is something I have come to think of as *alignment*. I feel like a musical instrument being played in tune by my Maker. It is wonderful.

Growing up, I didn't believe anything like this feeling of joyful alignment with myself and God was actually possible. No one explicitly taught me that it was impossible. They didn't sit me down and say, "Hey, Will, the Christian life—with all its talk of love, hope, forgiveness, and grace—doesn't feel a whole lot like those things. It mostly feels like we are holding out hope that one day Jesus will come back and make all of this mess better. Also, you are a mess. You might one day be slightly less a mess than you are now, but still, you will forever be a mess. But don't be hopeless! One day you will die, and then you won't be a mess anymore!"

I believed that every part of my life was infused with sin and brokenness, so it was logical to always look upon myself with distrust. It was as if I were always one step away from a cliff of my own making that I would somehow launch from someday. Probably by my own hand. Beware!

This is a tough way to live. I was in a constant position of guardedness toward my own self. Think about that. It would be as if I were to tell you, "Hey, great news: You can live in this incredible beachside mansion for free. It's yours! But somewhere in your new home is a deadly venomous snake that may strike at any moment. Enjoy the house!"

Maybe you understand this. Maybe you've always lived in that same kind of beach house. The worst kind of beach house.

No wonder so many of us go through life constantly looking over our shoulder for the next attack of sin rather than looking at the tremendous work of Christ in our lives.

I'm talking about the work of sanctification that the Holy Spirit does in us. The reality that we actually do grow and change! Things do get better! We do move on from those things that used to kick our butt. Our lives actually transform.

But many of us have been conditioned to look on the life of Christ as this thing that happened "out there" somewhere. It was thousands of years ago in a city we've never seen except on an episode of *The Chosen*. It's real. We do believe the story. But it is out there. His life is not something that could happen inside us. In our lives. In our innermost beings. In our thoughts, actions, and behaviors.

If we subconsciously subscribe to this "out there" way of thinking, we limit the power of God's ongoing grace and redemption in our lives. It is as if we have said, "Yes, God has the power to give me a ticket to heaven one day, but He has not given me the power to actually change right now."

What? Where in Scripture do we get this idea? Behold, the old has passed and the new has come (see 2 Cor. 5:17)! No, dear brother or sister, the Lord has given us all that we need to have a radically life-giving life. He has given us the life-giver Himself. Jesus Christ has sent the Spirit into our hearts to dwell within us. We keep acting like all we have is a one-hundred-watt bulb in us when actually the force of the risen sun dwells within our chest.

For most of my life, all I had was light-bulb belief. I was so committed to a certain concept about the size and power of sin that I missed the expansive nature of the gospel. I was limiting the power of ongoing grace in my life. It was as if I had made sin, and not redemption, the central theme of Scripture. Therefore, the central story of my own life was sin and not redemption.

What this practically meant was that I didn't think it was possible to actually experience ongoing, joyful alignment. Because a mess doesn't get to experience that much joy.

When I talk about alignment, I mean being in right relation with the triune God who made you. I also mean being aligned with your true self—the self *God made you to be*—and aligned with others in heart-connected relationships. To put it another way, if sin were like a dislocated shoulder, Christ's redemption is that arm being snapped back into place and given a completely new vitality. It's not even the same fragile joint anymore—it is healed and filled with strength!

I think many of us would say we believe this, but then we act like we don't think it is possible. When we don't actually believe it's possible, we stop looking to live that way. It turns out you can see only the door you are looking for.

Or to put it in the terms Jesus used, "Ask and it will be given to you; seek and you will find; knock and the door will be opened to you" (Luke 11:9 NIV). If you don't believe in the full and total life change that the miraculous life, death, and resurrection of Jesus promises for us, then why would you ever waste time asking, seeking, or knocking?

Remember the yellow car phenomenon in chapter 6? You suddenly see lots of yellow cars because you're thinking about them. This is like that but in reverse. You never look, so you never see. You never see, so you never experience. You never experience, so things never change.

To put it another way, if you didn't believe that drinking from a crisp mountain stream was possible because you couldn't conceive of a crisp mountain spring since you've never climbed a mountain before, you might settle for a mud puddle and think that was the best it could get. C. S. Lewis once said that it was as if we were a child who had thought a vacation was making mud pies in the gutter, not ever realizing that there was such a thing as a beach.[1]

Now, I know someone might have the temptation to think, *Oh, great—this is a book that says if I just had more faith, I would suddenly be experiencing more joy.* If that is where your head goes, you will either feel resentful toward me (please don't; I like you) or anger toward yourself for finding yet another way that you are "failing" (please don't do that either; you need to like you).

Instead, I'm inviting you to continue on this path of Spirit-led self-awareness with an ongoing sense of playful discovery and childlike wonder. Playfulness has to be infused in all of this or the temptation to turn back will be too strong. We will become evaluative, as if we are not learning something new but grading our homework. Have you ever learned something just for the raw wonder and joy of it? It feels completely different than studying it for a test. Please, find and hold on to that childlike wonder each step of the way.

How is this possible?

If you are a Christian, then right this second, the living Spirit of God abides in you. This Spirit of the Most High is nonstop inviting you into the most incredible thing in the world: union with God. This is an extension of the relationship that God already exists in—Father, Son, and Spirit. It is as if the best dance party ever is happening and you are invited *and* it turns out you are an incredible dancer with zero discomfort or self-evaluation.

My daughter dances like this—the joyful dance of a person who has yet to be mocked. The other day, I was teaching Penelope how to break asparagus stalks for dinner, and we were blasting some K-pop music in the background.

As you may know, the bottom of a stalk of fresh asparagus is this fibrous, rooty bit. Very hard to eat. You need to break it off before you put the rest in the oven. When you break the root, it often makes a satisfying snapping sound. Penelope took to this task with relish, dancing as she got the hang of it. "Look at this, Dad, I call this move the asparagus chop!" She began miming the breaking motion while doing her own version of the moonwalk across our kitchen floor. It was fantastic.

This is the kind of joyful dance we are called into. However, it is nearly impossible to step into this dance if we don't break free of the story that elevates sin over redemption. In order to do that, we have to stop believing ourselves to be solo beings. We are not alone, not now and not ever. The very Spirit who raised Christ from the dead is alive and at work within us. On those days when life is throwing curveball after curveball or bulldozing our house, the temptation is to look down at our own hands and say, "I cannot do it, so it cannot be done." This is a lie!

Now, instead of shaming yourself for feeling that way, and without doubling up on the internal monologue of shame (duet, anyone?), just be aware of it all. Just notice. Gently invite the Spirit to give you strength. Ask the Spirit to remind you of His power and presence. Remember that you are not alone. Just take four breaths to remember that. Can you hear it? Can you feel it? Can you accept it?

We can move in joyful alignment because we do not move alone.

> I have been crucified with Christ. It is no longer I
> who live, but Christ who lives in me. And the life I
> now live in the flesh I live by faith in the Son of God,
> who loved me and gave himself for me. (Gal. 2:20)

Let me get specific about coming into alignment in the context of relationships.

For a long time, I did not think my marriage could actually change. I would have said something like, "I think I'm ready for change, but I'm not sure we are both on the same timetable." This was me making an excuse for the state of our relationship. As if I were a victim in our marriage. I was often blaming Tiff.

But when I began to be enlivened in this new way by the power of the abiding Spirit, I was sustained in joy no matter what was happening with Tiff. I stopped blaming her for my own stuff. I could be with her and not take on her sorrow. I could love and serve her without making demands. I could simply love her. It was an echo of the love I was receiving from my good and gracious Father.

Anthony De Mello describes this kind of love as the shade of a tree. The tree does not demand that someone come sit in its shade, nor does it chase them down to come back to the shade. Neither does the tree force someone to change in order to be worthy of the shade. It just gives the shade.[2]

My love was beginning to be like this. Not always, but more and more over time.

The Lord was exposing me to a life that had seemed unfathomable to me even a few years before. The interesting thing was that, as joyful alignment came to define my life more every day, the context mattered less and less, and my desire for more joy grew stronger and stronger. It is like an upward spiral of supernaturally supplied hope, peace, and love.

As my vision got larger for what was possible in the power of the life of the Spirit, Tiff and I had an incredible conversation standing in the kitchen one day in that blurry moment after we had gotten the kids to sleep.

Me: Has blaming, shaming, or complaining ever helped our relationship? Or given us anything good?

Tiff: Umm ... no.

Me: But we have done it so much over the last eighteen years, right?

Tiff: Uh, yeah. For sure.

Me: I know I have blamed you for so much. I'm really sorry.

Tiff: Thanks for saying that. I know I have tried to shame you into change.

Me: Yeah, I have done that to you at least a thousand times.

Tiff: (laughing) That sounds close to accurate.

Me: Do we want to keep doing that?

Tiff: No ... I don't think so. I don't want that.

Me: Well, if it's never given us anything, would you say it's taken from us?

Tiff: Yeah, 100 percent.

Me: I don't want it to take from us anymore.

Tiff: So let's stop.

Me: Do you think we can just drop it? Like, make a commitment to each other to drop blame/shame/ complain from our relationship and it just be gone?

Tiff: I think so.

Me: Let's try.

So we did. We stood there in our kitchen and made a verbal commitment to each other to drop blame/shame/complain from our marriage. The craziest thing? It happened. Ninety percent of our blame/shame/complain behavior was gone immediately.

Now, when we notice it happening, we simply name it.

> **Tiff:** I feel like you might be shaming me right now. Is that a story I'm telling myself, or is that right?
>
> **Me:** Oh ... let me check in with myself. (long pause) No, I'm not. I'm sorry you are feeling that. What did I say that sparked shame for you?

Or:

> **Me:** Let me check in with myself. (long pause) Yes. Yes, I'm trying to shame you. I'm feeling afraid right now, and I went into protection mode. Please forgive me. Can I tell you why I was afraid?

Now, such moments don't happen in a vacuum. By this point, Tiff and I had both done intensive trauma therapy work, separately and together. Tiff was also working with an incredible counselor and psychiatrist who had helped get her the right treatment and meds for her depression. And I had logged more than one thousand hours of morning prayer and meditation. We would *not* have been able to even propose this idea without all that work.

And to double down on my earlier point, I would not have been able to even propose this idea without believing that it was possible through the abiding power of the Spirit of God. If we believe something is impossible, we don't even bother looking for it.

We also would not have been able to take this step without changing our attitude toward judgment.

Jesus famously said, "First take the log out of your own eye, and then you will see clearly to take the speck out of your brother's eye" (Matt. 7:5). I don't know about you, but I kind of glaze over when I read that verse. It has become such a go-to reference about judgment that I'm not sure we really grasp the radical nature of it. At least, I didn't.

I'd heard it in sermons, Sunday school classes, and podcasts, and yet I was still so good at judging others. Judgment for me was a deeply ingrained habit that moved outward in concentric circles, starting with the judgment I gave myself, followed by judgment of those closest to me, from whom I demanded the most. The circles expanded outward from there, until ultimately my judgment included the whole world.

I judge me. I judge you too, my family and friends. In the end, I judge the world at large.

When you judge someone, you lose the ability to see them. This is true of someone else, just as it is true of yourself. Judgment assumes that you know what is right and wrong, that you are accurately assessing truth, and it carries with it a solution or next step.

But what if, instead of judgment, what all the people in those circles need is compassion and healing? Maybe this is what we would see if we took the log of judgment out of our eye.

This kind of seeing is not blind. It does not evaluate but takes in reality as it is. This kind of seeing is patient, gentle, kind, and good because it is infused with love and joy from the always-abiding love of Christ.

When we become assured of this love, we stop evaluating ourselves as if we might somehow lose God's acceptance. We can realistically see our many follies, missteps, and sins through eyes of healing love, not self-condemnation.

After all, "There is therefore now no condemnation for those who are in Christ Jesus" (Rom. 8:1). Are you in Christ? If so, why would you still condemn yourself?

Instead, take the plank out of your own eye and look upon yourself with compassion and really see. As you learn to do this, you will begin to extend this healing eye toward those around you.[3]

Soon after Tiffany and I began to do this with each other, we felt the difference. We didn't speak with the same heat. Our conversations no longer felt like one of us had to be the winner. We are both Enneagram eights, which means we challenge everything. We litigate everything. Prior to this shift, I think our baseline style of communication was "MMA fight."

We noticed that as we moved toward each other with the plank removed from our own eyes, the most marvelous thing happened: We didn't see the speck in each other's eye. We saw each other.

The speck says, "He should," "She should," and "They should." He should stop being so _____. She should get a handle on _____. He should be more _____. I wish she were less _____.

But when the plank is gone, and therefore the speck doesn't matter to us anymore, we say, feel, and believe, "He is," "She is," and "They are." These are statements of acceptance.

And acceptance feels like a willingness to be with them *as they are*, in love.

In our current cultural moment, we confuse acceptance with approval. Our culture says that to be with someone in full reality, seeing them as they are and being fully with them (actual presence), is to say, "I approve of all the choices you have made." But to remove the plank from your own eye and move through the world without judging those around you is not the equivalent of approval. After all, approval is still a judgment.

This kind of acceptance is another way of loving your neighbor (see Matt. 22:39). It is another way of weeping with those who weep and rejoicing with those who rejoice (see Rom. 12:15). It is another way of saying that the love of Christ—the all-healing, all-forgiving love of Christ—is with us now.

The friendship Tiff and I shared began to feel like sacred ground. And I would not have been able to conceive of a relationship with this much tenderhearted connection without the work of the abiding Spirit.

To put it another way, you don't know how spectacular the view is unless you start climbing the mountain. Then, once you see that first vista, you start to wonder, *What does it look like farther up?* You get inspired to keep walking the path. The Lord in His mercy had me hungry for the next bend in the path. There was still no elevator to the peak of Mt. Everest, but there was a route.

If we don't believe that alignment with self and our Maker is actually possible, we will not seek it. We will spiritually settle. As if the psalmist said that we would walk *only* in the valley of the shadow of death. If we believe this, we will never look for the still waters He would lead us along. We will never seek the pasture. We will emotionally and mentally decide that it is not possible.

PRACTICE: Alignment

1. Get still. Breathe.
2. Get curious—does it feel impossible to live a life of alignment with yourself, or do you feel a wellspring of hope and wonder?
3. Don't judge what comes up—simply notice it.
4. Take a few minutes to write out what you notice. If such an alignment feels impossible, ask the Spirit to bring you into awareness and understanding of *why* it feels impossible. Is there any underlying belief or a subconscious commitment you've made that is no longer useful? If you begin to feel hope and wonder welling up, stay with it. What is the Lord putting on your heart? Do you find your attitude softening toward yourself? Do you feel

yourself softening toward someone you've been sitting in judgment over?

5. Repeat this practice every day for a week. See what comes up over many days of nonjudgmental curiosity about alignment.

PRACTICE: Judgment

1. Get still. Breathe.

2. Ask yourself this question: "Am I sitting in judgment on someone in my life right now?"

3. As a person comes to the surface of your thoughts, fill in the blank of this sentence:

He should _____.

She should _____.

He should stop being so _____.

She should get a handle on _____.

They should be more _____.

4. Just notice that all of this came up without self-condemnation. Simply be aware.

5. Ask the Spirit to soften your heart toward this person. Ask the Spirit to move you toward seeing them as they are and loving them right where they are.

6. At this point, I find it helpful to write out a "reality" statement of acceptance. "He should" becomes "He is."

For example, I reached out to a certain friend for help with Raylan on three separate occasions. I felt vulnerable in sharing my need. At first, he had reasons why the timing wasn't right. This happened twice. I got judgy and hurt. Finally, I asked him point-blank, "Why aren't you helping me?" He told me he didn't know how, and he didn't think he could dedicate the kind of time and space it would take to come alongside us. Initially, I was even more hurt. I felt like:

He should help us.

He should care more.

He is failing me.

However, over time I came to accept my friend's clearly stated limitations. As I did, I found my judgment and anger melting away. I was able to see him as he was, not as I wished him to be. I decided I still wanted to be his friend, and friends with the actual person, not my hoped-for, idealized version.

––––––––––

Chapter 10

Scarcity

This mantra of *not enough* carries the day and
becomes a kind of default setting.

Lynne Twist, *The Soul of Money*

I was afraid, and I went and hid
your talent in the ground.

Matthew 25:25

True story: The roof is leaking, we've just discovered a nest of rats in our crawl space, and our hatchback, a model built only one year, is dying.

It did not occur to me when we purchased this particular model of hatchback to wonder why it was made for only one year. Perhaps not a good sign? It is already zip-tied together, and now the transmission is shot.

The thing about caring for a loved one with a disability is that it can feel like you are always almost out of money. It seems like it doesn't matter how much you have on any given day, there is always another medical bill right around the corner. There is this sense of financially holding your breath, waiting for the other shoe to drop. Clearly, this is not my son's fault. This is just the nature of needing ongoing medical attention.

Now three shoes have dropped, and one of them is full of rats.

I was really scared.

On the journey of Spirit-led self-awareness, I have found over and over again that there is resistance to seeking this kind of understanding. In other words, you don't *really* want to know what is going on in there. To look inside consistently requires that you have the bravery of someone committed to honest change. As they say in AA, all progress starts with the truth.

One of the truths I came to realize as I walked out daily self-awareness practices was how afraid I was about money. My belief went like this: there is never enough, and what little there is will be gone faster than we can replace it.

Where did this belief come from?

When I was a kid, we were a family on a mission. My dad and mom had moved our small family from the familiarity of North Carolina up to the frigid coastline of Massachusetts so my dad could go to seminary. We were the only people on our block who served sweet tea or ate grits at every breakfast. The plan was to go to seminary and then head straight back to the South. But my dad was inspired by the church-planting movement of the early eighties, so after lots of prayer and conversations with my mom, they decided we were going to stay.

As a kid, I had no context for any of this. All I knew was that my dad was starting a church in the office of a gas station. The kind of church where you brought your own folding chair and/or tambourine. My dad now says it was not in the office of a gas station but rather a car wash, as if this distinction changes the grittiness of this gospel adventure. It does not.

It was wild, intense, and full of crazy highs as we watched this little church go from thirty folks to nearly two thousand by the mid-1990s.

What it was not full of was money.

Now, don't get me wrong: At no point was I in danger of missing a meal or not having clothes on my back. My parents were faithful providers of all the basics. There just wasn't much margin. I remember for the longest time we had this huge freezer in our garage that someone had given us. It was always empty. Then one day, a friend visiting from the South filled it with frozen hamburger meat and chicken, and it was like manna from heaven. It was a big deal to have all this extra food.

Like most parents, mine did not hand me a philosophy of money or a theological analysis of how to approach financial resources. My siblings and I picked it up through that unique childhood osmosis of watching and listening to things you don't really understand. You gather bits and pieces over time, forming your own philosophy in your head. You subtly pick up on what is considered right and wrong. Used minivan? That is okay to own. Volvo? Nope, too nice for a pastor. If your car can be on the verge of breaking down at all times, all the better.

That one is no joke. We had a minivan for a long time that would stop functioning anytime it rained for longer than seven minutes. If this happened on a road trip to North Carolina, my dad would pull over and take a piece of cardboard he carried for this purpose and place it over the engine as a water barrier. He would then close the hood of the car, start the engine back up, and resume driving with what to my young mind could only be described as the worst plan B ever. However, *MacGyver* was a hit show at the time, so maybe this was just creative?

As we got older and saw that our friends were taking vacations or getting a car when they turned sixteen, my mom would say, "We would absolutely do that too if we could, but we are a family in ministry, and it's just not possible." The subtext being something like, "We are poor for Jesus, and that is the right way to follow Him."

This sort of thing, combined with the occasional judgy comment about someone else's car or lifestyle, and you can see how my childhood mind formed a map that had money at one end and Jesus on the other. No one intentionally taught me this, but what I took away from my childhood was that you needed to be poor in order to really be Christlike.

I was that kid who was baptized at six, first read through the whole Bible by nine, and couldn't wait to become a youth group leader as soon as someone would hand him an acoustic guitar. I wanted to be Christlike so badly. A wonderful thing. I didn't understand that I had turned my parents' unexplained financial choices into my own system of beliefs that would subconsciously guide me for decades to come.

Those beliefs went something like this:

- There is never enough.
- There is no such thing as righteous wealth.
- If you start to feel you have enough, what that really means is you have too much.
- And because there is no such thing as righteous wealth, you should feel really guilty and make bad financial decisions until you feel like you don't have enough again.
- Yet, in a classic example of a catch-22, you'll really feel safe only if you have enough.
- Repeat cycle.

It's important that you see that this was happening subconsciously and that it was driven by beliefs, leading to feelings, leading to actions. The belief part is key. What that really means is that the actual financial number doesn't matter. I could have a million dollars in the bank, and I'd still wake up with that tightness in my chest whispering words of fear. My perception of safety was not driven by a number but a feeling of not-enough-ness. (That is the technical term, I think.)

I'm not alone in this cycle of scarcity thinking. One of my friends built a company from the ground up that is consistently profitable after thirteen years in business. He has employed dozens of local people and helped them have great financial lives. However, every time he has to make a big inventory purchase, he gets sick to his stomach thinking this is the moment when he screws it all up and goes back to being broke. He feels unsafe.

Another friend, by far the most financially successful person I know, sold his company worth hundreds of millions of dollars. He still obsessively checks his accounts and wonders how to cut costs in his life. When I asked him about this tendency, he echoed that familiar statement—the other shoe can drop at any moment. He is aware that he lives with abundance in the bank and scarcity in his heart. Scarcity is not related to a number.

Circumstantial changes don't seem to affect this underlying subconscious cycle for me and others. The nuances might be different for you, but my pattern is like this:

There is not enough.	I must get more to be safe.	Now I have too much.	Self-sabotage in guilt.	Repeat pattern.

I have friends whose patterns run more like this:

There is not enough.	I must get more to be safe.	I get more.	I still don't feel safe, so it must be that I still don't have enough.	Go get more.	Repeat pattern.

Or:

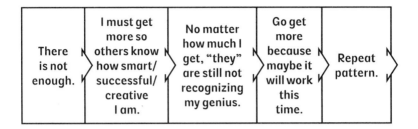

There is not enough.	I must get more so others know how smart/successful/creative I am.	No matter how much I get, "they" are still not recognizing my genius.	Go get more because maybe it will work this time.	Repeat pattern.

Now, there are many theologians and spiritual teachers who would stop you at this point and say, "The problem is you, you awful sinner who can't seem to put Jesus first. If you didn't have money as an idol, you'd be fine. But you continue to worship money." At which point, you'd add another layer of guilt upon your life with no further clarity about what to actually do with the underlying issues that you simply don't know how to bring to the surface. I will not do that to you.

The gift of Spirit-led self-awareness is that we get to move toward understanding and insight into the patterns that are like underwater currents moving us this way and that. Like a ship tossed about by the waves. Self-awareness in and through the Spirit gives us an anchor in the storm. We begin to ask, "How should I live in regard to resources?" And we ask this question with a tenderness toward self, remembering that the kindness of the Lord is what brings about repentance. Be kind to yourself here, my friend.

Now, since this is not a financial advice book, you won't get any clear wisdom from me on tithing or how much to put in your IRA. However, what I am imminently concerned about is living in constant and total peace in the Lord no matter your financial circumstances.

Even saying it like that sounds laughable. As if I just said, "What I really care about is your ability to dunk a basketball, though you're just five-two." This is where the claims of Jesus and Paul get really interesting.

First, we have Paul saying:

> Not that I am speaking of being in need, for I have learned in whatever situation I am to be content. I know how to be brought low, and I know how to abound. In any and every circumstance, I have learned the secret of facing plenty and hunger, abundance and need. I can do all things through him who strengthens me. (Phil. 4:11–13)

Paul is declaring, as boldly as he can, that there is a way to live in peace with a lot *or* a little. What an insane statement for an American Christian to hear in the twenty-first century.

The part of this passage that feels even wilder to me is that he goes back and forth between these two states: having plenty, having nothing. I think humans can adapt to a lot of different things, especially if we have time to adjust to the new situation. We can tighten the belt, eat more ramen, budget ourselves to death, and figure out how to live on a shoestring budget. Simultaneously, I'm pretty sure we could somehow get used to having lots of money. It reminds me of the old joke: "Money can't buy you happiness, but it can buy you a Jet Ski, and have you ever seen someone sad on a Jet Ski?"*

---

* This is often attributed to Daniel Tosh, but is sometimes debated as to which comedian said it first.

But to move back and forth between poverty and wealth throughout your life and yet maintain true contentment? Paul is seriously dialed into his inner well-being. How?

He points to his mystical union with Jesus. He can do this, and in fact "all things," through Christ who strengthens him. It is worth double-clicking on this idea. He is saying that he, Paul, a living, breathing person like you and me, is so tapped in to the life of Christ who *dwells in him* that a by-product of this indwelling is contentment in all sorts of financial situations. Incredible!

Also, he is saying that staying tuned in to contentment is so hard that he cannot do it on his own. Only the fool thinks that contentment is easy to get and keep. Paul is arguing that it requires the supernatural indwelling power of the Most High God.

In other words, untangling ourselves from the grip of scarcity thinking is so hard that it requires an act of God.

Unfortunately, Paul doesn't give us an easy-to-use, step-by-step guide. He didn't provide any three-step sermon formulas or handy alliteration to make our note-taking easier. But I think there's a spot a little earlier in the chapter where Paul gives us a very strong clue to the way he thinks *and* takes action on this concept:

> The Lord is at hand; do not be anxious about anything, but in everything by prayer and supplication with thanksgiving let your requests be made known to God. And the peace of God, which surpasses all understanding, will guard your hearts and your minds in Christ Jesus. (vv. 5b–7)

Recall the pattern we've discussed: beliefs shape emotions, and our emotions shape our actions. Let's break it down a little more.

First, Paul's belief: "The Lord is at hand." Paul writes these words at a moment when Jesus is *not* physically there holding his hand. Paul writes this in the same way you and I might say it today. Paul's belief is that the Lord is indwelling his very person, living within him!

Next, we get a glimpse of the emotions that Paul is writing about here: Paul says he feels thanksgiving, or what we might think of as gratitude. Have you ever felt true gratitude? It is an incredible emotion. It is like joy that wants to give a hug to everyone. Gratitude is wonderful! But how can Paul feel gratitude *before* he gets what he is praying for—and not even knowing if he will get what he's praying for? Because his gratitude is grounded in his belief that the Lord is already at hand. His belief is shaping his emotions!

Third, the actions that Paul recommends: prayer and supplication. Paul is asking God for all sorts of things and then acting as if he has already received whatever the best thing for him might be at that exact moment. How do we know that? Because he tells us that the peace of God is guarding his heart and mind. Here again we have mystical union language from Paul. He goes out of his way to let us know that our rational mind, the part of us that always wants a simple logic map, will not comprehend what's going on here. The experience will in fact "surpass all understanding." What an incredible life Paul invites us into!

Next, we have the bananas-crazy words of Jesus Himself. I want to set the stage for you a bit. Jesus was speaking to an agrarian society of farmers, shepherds, and low-wage earners who were always one bad harvest away from severe consequences, like starvation. And yet to this audience Jesus speaks these famous words:

> Look at the birds of the air: they neither sow nor reap nor gather into barns, and yet your heavenly Father feeds them.... Consider the lilies of the field, how they grow: they neither toil nor spin, yet I tell you, even Solomon in all his glory was not arrayed like one of these.... Therefore do not be anxious about tomorrow, for tomorrow will be anxious for itself. Sufficient for the day is its own trouble. (Matt. 6:26, 28b–29, 34)

Either Jesus was the most oblivious public speaker in the history of the world and simply didn't understand His audience *or* He actually knew that this kind of life was possible.

Can you imagine being on the razor's edge of starvation from a drought you didn't anticipate and then hearing Jesus basically say, "Don't worry about it—God's got you"? I'd be like, "Read the room, Jesus!" To be honest, I think I'd dismiss Him as some prosperity-gospel, self-help guru who did not have enough real-world experience to earn my trust. And yet God is asking us to step past our wounds and cynicism into something incredible: a life of peace.

When was the last time you worried about money? If you said, "Nine seconds ago," you are not alone. Recent data by the Decision Lab found that 77 percent of Americans feel anxious about their financial situation.[1] And yet, if we were to actually believe Jesus' words and live this out as our daily reality despite the circumstances of our life, can you imagine the amount of freedom we would feel every day?

The immediate question for me again is, "How do I live this way, Jesus? How do I internally take hold of this incredible life You are describing?" It cannot be through the context-based promises of the world. Wealth management companies market "peace of mind" by implying that they can make it so you will have a ton of money for retirement. That is their answer to this conundrum: if you just save enough, then one day you won't have this kind of anxiety.

But Jesus doesn't say, "If you want to lose all anxiety, just start putting money away so you will have enough to live off for twenty or so years, adjusted for inflation." Now, I am not saying that you should not have a retirement fund—but it will never offer you spiritual peace.

So what will? Jesus says the most remarkable thing: "Look at the birds." Amazing. Have you looked at a bird lately? They are incredible, and they seem to be doing whatever they want all the time. Have you noticed that? One minute, they are singing. Another minute, they're chasing another bird in what looks to be some sort of aerial ballet. A few seconds later, they are hopping on the ground grabbing a bug and looking pretty pleased with themselves.

This blows my mind because it does not line up with one of my core values in life: work hard, and when in doubt, work harder. Now, I'm not knocking hard work. It's great, and I love it so much (ask my wife and friends). But Jesus is saying that your own hard work is *not* the way to get this kind of peace. How do we know this? Hear the words of Jesus again:

> Look at the birds of the air: they neither sow nor reap
> nor gather into barns, and yet your heavenly Father
> feeds them. (Matt. 6:26)

They neither sow nor reap nor gather into barns. In other words, the bird is not busting his tail feathers nonstop to produce and store away. Yet he still has peace. We might say this another way: The bird's peace comes from his absolute trust that his Maker is for him and will provide. His trust is not grounded in his own efforts but on the providence of the Most High.

Yet another way to put this might be: if God owns the cattle on a thousand hills, we don't have to (see Ps. 50:10).

Our peace comes before our having anything. Peace comes before having. Do you want to live counterculturally in this modern moment? Try that one out.

Jesus closes this section with an incredible statement: "Do not be anxious for tomorrow." I love those moments in Scripture when it is so clear that Jesus knows the hearts of mankind. This is one of them. He knows that where you find scarcity beliefs, catastrophic thinking is not far off.

Catastrophic thinking is that tendency to look into the future and imagine calamity after calamity. The worst is not only likely but certain. Scarcity thinking says, "There is *not* enough now, and there will be even less tomorrow!"

It is fascinating to me that I got so good at catastrophic thinking and that I embraced it with a level of certainty I have never held for any positive thinking. For example, if I get a leaky tire on my car, I instantly assume there is a nail in it, I'll have to buy four new tires within the next forty-eight hours, *and* an out-of-nowhere medical bill will arrive right after that. My palms begin to sweat, my heart races, and I'm certain that this is what is going to happen. Mentally and emotionally, I am no longer in the present; I'm out there in this tragic future that I'm so sure will happen.

The fascinating part is I can do that easily, but I've never been this certain of any positive outcome. I've never thought, *Ooh, a flat tire probably means I will have to spend only fifteen bucks at AutoZone to buy a plug kit. And maybe they're having a sale!*

Yet time after time, God has proven Himself faithful to me.

Did I mention the rats? The thing you might not know about rat infestations, unless you (like us) have played host to what the experts call a *rat-breeding den of iniquity*, is that they are nearly impossible to get rid of. I tried all the home remedies I learned on YouTube, and I think this only made them angry.

I finally had to call in a pro, Mike the Rat Guy. This is not my name for Mike. This is how he put his contact info into my phone. What he recommended was to dig a trench around the entire house, bury some chicken wire, cover that with cement, *and then* install traps everywhere to kill the rest. This is a multi-week, labor-intensive project.

If you've learned anything about me so far, you'll know that I was full-on panicking about how we were going to pay for any of this. But the same week I got the quote from Mike the Rat Guy, we got a random check in the mail. Out of nowhere. My old Sunday school teacher from third grade simply felt that the Lord had told him and his wife to send us the check for whatever we needed it for (may his name be blessed). Tiff and I laughed and cried. The amount on the check was enough to get rid of the rats.

So you'd think I would've learned something from that, wouldn't you? Did I mention that the roof was leaking?

A few weeks later, a friend took me to coffee with his mentor, whom I hadn't previously met. As we got to know each other, I was raw and honest about the intensity of our lives. We had one of those genuine moments of connection, what I'd later think of as full presence, and he prayed over me before we left.

A few days later, my friend called. He said his mentor didn't want to make a big deal about it, but he was going to take care of the roof. We never saw an invoice.

A few weeks after that, I was getting ready to fly to Florida to buy a used Kia Sportage from my brother. He is in the automotive industry and can usually find great deals through his network. Tiff and I figured out a way to put some money down, and then we'd have a monthly car payment. We would make it work. Then yet another friend found out about this plan, and he told me, "I don't want y'all to have to deal with all of that. I know you have a lot of other expenses." As he said this, he handed me a check for the total price of the Kia.

It was incredible. We experienced a wave of awe and gratitude. Simple shock in the face of God's goodness. Tiff and I danced, we laughed, we prayed, and I fist-pumped every time I got into that Kia.

This euphoric faith lasted a good month or so, before I began to notice my fear beginning to creep back in. *God took care of us this time, but what about next time and the time after that?*

I decided that I needed to learn to practice the kind of contentment that Paul had, that Jesus promises, and that God provides.

PRACTICE: What Is My Money Story?

How do we practice Paul's contentment? Try this practice for the next seven days, and see what you learn. This exercise is best done at a consistent time each day or night, whichever feels right to you. I personally practice this one in the morning, but your mileage may vary.

1. Get still. Let your body and mind settle. Breathe.
2. Fill in the blank: "As I think about money, I feel _____." It might be helpful to reframe this question to, "As I think about money, I notice _____ happening in my body." For example, for a while as I thought about money, I noticed the tightening in my chest that indicates rising stress.
3. Notice what comes up—but without self-condemnation or judgment. Simply notice the feeling. Is it gratitude? Joy? Sadness? Fear? Anxiety? Maybe even dread?

4 Get curious with the following questions. It may help to journal them out:

- What could cause me to experience this feeling?
- What stories about money am I living out of?
- Did I make those up myself, or were they handed to me? If they were handed to me in my family, do I remember when and how that happened?
- Do I feel at peace with the way I'm living in regard to financial resources? If not, where is the friction point?

The goal of this practice is simple insight into self. You are not trying to approach yourself like a problem to be solved; you are just learning. Do this for seven days, and just notice what you notice. Let it come to the surface. At the end of the seven days, look back at your journal entries. Are there any patterns or themes? Any beliefs or commitments made subconsciously that are no longer useful or important to your life? Is there something new you feel called to step into? Something old you need to let go of?

Whenever the Spirit brings to light something I hadn't been aware of before, I have found it helpful to share it with someone who loves me. Talking it out with them often reveals concrete and practical next steps I can take. It is one thing to say, "I want to let go of this self-shaming story I had about money from childhood." It is another to have a friend walk with you as you explore next steps.

For example, Tiff and I never had a good savings plan for Raylan's future, and I felt tons of shame about that. So much so that I just avoided the topic. But as the shame came to light and the Lord met me with His unending love, I talked with a close friend about the entire experience. He helped me work out the details of a retirement plan that would include three people, not just Tiff and me. This feels like wisdom, but we are not asking this retirement plan to give us spiritual peace.

PRACTICE: Appreciation

In her book *The Soul of Money*, Lynne Twist develops an amazing idea that can be expressed like this: "What you appreciate, appreciates."[2] In other words, what you give your attention to takes up more space in your thoughts and emotions, and can even impact your behavior.

For the next seven days, keep an appreciation journal. Here is how it works:

1. Write down a moment when God gave you exactly what you needed in your life. Maybe this was food, maybe medicine, maybe clothing. Maybe loving companionship. Maybe just breath and water that day. Whatever it is, can you see it as a gift?

2. After you write it down, close your eyes and do a simple four-count breathing exercise while meditating on this gift. Can you appreciate how God

has provided for you sufficiently in this right-now moment? As this feeling of appreciation rises, simply notice it. Bring your full attention to it.

That's it. Rinse and repeat every day for a week and see if your ability to appreciate what God is doing right this second begins to change.

———————

Chapter 11

Flow

It's as though we're stuck in a hole
and the only tools our culture throws
us are an assortment of shovels.

Richard Schwartz, *You Are the One You've Been Waiting For*

I love work. In my battery-acid days, before trauma camp, before
learning how to walk out a daily practice of Spirit-led self-awareness,
work was often the only place where I saw myself as effective and
capable. I could go to work, set a goal, push forward to make it happen
... and see results! At home, it felt like I was pushing a lawn mower
with no blade. Row after row of nothing changing.

So it made sense that work became a place of enjoyment and even
respite. But over time, I could see that my identity was starting to be
shaped around it. I was only ever as good as my results at work. When
things at home felt like an emotional dumpster fire, it was the most
natural thing in the world to seek validation elsewhere. This is what I
was doing. I started to think that if the results at work were awesome,

then I was awesome. If my results at work didn't meet my ever-growing expectations, then everything was miserable. I had stumbled into work codependency.

Way back in 2007, Tiffany and I had moved into a historically low-income neighborhood in Nashville in order to develop what I would come to call a *theology of neighbor*. We wanted to learn how to love our neighbors as we loved ourselves—not in a theoretical way or on a one-off mission trip, but as a daily lifestyle. We didn't know how to do that without just moving in and showing up as learners.

Tiff, who is considerably tougher than me, got a job "behind bars" as a job-training specialist for former offenders. She went to work every day at Charles Bass men's prison. Her goal was to equip justice-involved neighbors to find employment when they came home. Transitioning back to the community is one of the most challenging things for this population, and having a stable job to come home to provides a storm shelter in the midst of a tornado of change.

Her work was beautiful, hard, and redemptive. She came home absolutely spent. It also happened that she was coming home to the same neighborhood that many of the men she worked with were from. They and their families were our neighbors.

We had an open-door policy at our house. Justice-involved friends were at our house all the time, sharing meals, birthdays, Thanksgiving, and Christmas.

We started doing fun things with some of the teenagers in the community, like re-creating the NBA playoffs on the Xbox with a first-place prize of $50. (Side note: If you want to see focused teenagers, offer cash prizes for video game wins.) We put toys on the front porch, and a friend built us a free mini-library next to the mailbox. Pretty soon, our house was bustling at all hours. Eventually, we bought a Closed/Open sign for the door to let the kids know that snack hour did not extend to 10:00 p.m.

It was a season of learning. Repeatedly, Tiff and I were retaught how to weep with those who weep and rejoice with those who rejoice. God revealed to us so many of our biases, assumptions, and uninvestigated beliefs that were based more on historical racism than kingdom-minded grace. We began to learn how to truly love our neighbors. It's a lesson we continue to walk out to this day, as we are still living in that community where we've been for eighteen years.

One of the consistent patterns we saw with many of our neighbors and friends was that economic challenges have a domino effect. Your car breaks down and you can't afford to get it fixed until the next payday, so you take the bus. The bus is always a little late, so now you are late to work. You lose your job, can't fix the car, and it is very hard to get to the next job interview without reliable transportation. Meanwhile, your mom needs to move in for health reasons, and that is going to stretch your already considerably stretched resources.

We saw over and over again our incredible neighbors working multiple jobs and doing many things to make their economic lives work. We started to wonder if God was calling us to walk alongside our neighbors in a new way. We began to pray.

Our neighbors are fellow image bearers uniquely reflecting the glory of the Most High God. This means they are worthy of dignity, honor, and respect, of course. But it also means that they have God-given passions, creativity, and drive. Just like me. Just like you. In other words, the problem behind so many of the financial issues they were experiencing was not lack of talent or drive but lack of opportunity. So in 2011 we launched Corner to Corner, a nonprofit ministry designed to build a bridge of opportunity into the marketplace.

Over many years and through many iterations of learning and growth, we ultimately created a program called The Academy, which equips underestimated entrepreneurs with the tools to plan, start, and grow their own small businesses. We started at the local rec center around the corner from our house, and we have now scaled to thirteen locations in and around Nashville. As of this writing, we've launched more than twelve hundred entrepreneurs, and our goal is to launch ten thousand.[*]

One of these incredible neighbors is my friend Adrienne Bowling. Adrienne had a brilliant idea to become the "Uber of notaries."[†] The availability of notaries can seem almost laughably limited, as if they only work fourteen minutes every third Tuesday. Adrienne saw the need for a mobile, on-demand notary service and decided to fill the gap in the market.

In its first year, A-1 Mobile Notary did $35,000 worth of business. That's an awesome success, especially considering Adrienne had no formal business training. But her growth stalled out, and she started looking for accessible resources in the neighborhood. That's when she found Corner to Corner.

After going through our training program, her revenue jumped to $85,000 in the next twelve months. She was so encouraged by her experience that she came back and became one of our facilitators,

---

[*]   According to data from the SBA, these entrepreneurs will put, on average, $250 million back into the neighborhood economy!

[†]   A notary is a person who has to legally cosign important documents pertaining to things like home purchases and wills.

teaching the next group of entrepreneurs how to launch successfully. When asked about what her business growth has meant to her, she said, "Entrepreneurship broke the chains of poverty in my life. It has meant everything! I was able to get my family a bunch of amazing opportunities, including a new education path for my kids. My business is changing their lives and mine. Entrepreneurship taught me how to put a value on my time and on my skills that really has no limit."

The best part of this whole thing is that Adrienne's own God-given passion, creativity, and drive are the real source of her success.

In 2024 our graduates put an estimated $33.3 million back into the neighborhood economy.[1] It has been a wild ride.

In the months after trauma camp, the initial focus of my self-awareness work was at home. Learning to be present for Tiff, Raylan, and Penelope. Learning how to rest in the abiding love of my heavenly Father. Learning to listen and move *with* the Spirit. Learning to trust in my identity as one of the beloved.

However, after a few months of total home-related focus, I began to shift my attention to work. Work occupies one-third of the average American's life.[2] Think about that. So if it feels important to concentrate on what you do for a living, I would argue that it should. Anything that you are going to do for a third of your life should hopefully be done with joy and intention.

However, in my own Christian subculture, I'd learned two confusing things about work. The first was that I should do all things to the glory of God (see 1 Cor. 10:31b). In one sense, of course, this is a great scriptural truth. What I interpreted it to mean, though, was that I should work really hard and hold myself to a standard of excellence that was nearly impossible to hold every day. When I inevitably fall short of that, I should feel like a failure who has let God down.

The second confusing thing I'd learned was that I could *not* make work an idol. If I did that, then I was way off track and would be like the bad dad from every eighties or nineties film who neglected his kids and wife and didn't know the true meaning of Christmas. See 1994's *The Santa Clause* for Exhibit A. To be a workaholic dad was to be the lowest of the low.

This set about an internal conflict that led to workaholic tendencies coupled with intense self-induced shame and a vague unease that I wasn't doing work right.

All of this was happening in a larger cultural context in America that we could call a *meritocracy*. This is just a hundred-dollar word that means you are only as worthy as what you are doing or producing. We treat people this way all the time. If you are a doctor, lawyer, CEO, etc., you instantly have tremendous respect because you are out there killing it! Way to go! If you have a lower-paying job or are in some way not "performing" up to your full potential or to the standards of the most successful, then we dismiss you as not worthy of our attention. What you do gives you your merit. Hence, meritocracy.

We Christians are not past making this same mistake. I have known business leaders who look like success on paper but whose personal lives are openly on fire, and yet they are still asked to be elders at their church. One of them shared with me, in pure bafflement, "Don't they know what is really happening in my life?"

I decided that I needed a completely new relationship with work. What was my goal? I wanted to experience as much joy and alignment with self, God, and others as possible, all while doing work that was deeply meaningful to me and blessed the world.

One quick point: The work didn't have to be meaningful by anyone else's standards. I didn't want to be chasing the definition of success I got from my mom or dad, for example. It had to be meaningful to me. I didn't want to live out anyone else's story anymore.

So where to start with this wild goal?

The first thing I did was simply ask myself if I still felt aligned with my work at Corner to Corner. I wanted to know whether the job still felt in tune with my sense of purpose, my skills, and the opportunities before me. I didn't answer this quickly. I let the question settle in over many days. I brought it to the Lord in daily contemplative prayer, not so much asking for an immediate answer but rather sitting with the question in the presence of the Spirit. Anytime I noticed a sense of panic or urgency around this question, like I had to solve it *fast*, I just noticed the feeling, gave it space, and let it go.

Over time, a gentle yes percolated to the surface. Yes, this is the work I am meant to put my hands on fully in this season. I felt like a farmer grabbing hold of the handles of an old plow. It felt honest, true, and right. It felt simple.

One of the stories I was able to let go of permanently at this time was the myth that I am called to do only one thing forever. Have you ever felt that way? In Christian circles, we often talk about someone's *calling*, as if all of us are meant to have a burning bush moment like Moses did that dictates the rest of our lives. But as far as I can tell from reading my Bible, the burning bush happened only once.

What if we are called to one kind of work for a season and then God will call us toward another work for another season? What if this looked like natural growth rather than failure or losing our identity? I think we could rightly argue that even Moses didn't have just one calling. First, he was a son of Pharaoh, raised to help run an empire. Then he became a shepherd, husband, and father. Then he was a miracle-working deliverer who led the Israelites out of Egypt. Then he was a desert navigator, camp counselor, and hope instigator. Over the course of his life, he was also a battle commander, lawgiver, judge, and HR manager for one of the world's first org charts (see Ex. 18:21).

When I stepped out of the story that calling meant I was just one thing, I felt forever freed. I felt as if I could stay in tune with the Spirit while also doing really good work with what the Lord had put before me *right now*. And later, maybe He would lead me to other work. It was a wonderful experience.

It is not lost on me that when I began to ask my work-alignment questions, I already had a ton of autonomy and freedom. This is one of the benefits of being a social entrepreneur, and I know it is not the norm. I do not take that lightly or for granted.

That said, it is a false idea that we don't have a choice with our work. I have seen many people get into a "stuck loop," feeling like they are trapped in a particular job because of all sorts of reasons. When we approach our work from a place of "I am stuck and there is nothing

I can do," we are back on the drama triangle. If you find yourself in this space, simply notice it. Don't shame yourself for feeling this way. Move toward tenderhearted self-curiosity. See if God is trying to bring something to your awareness. It is okay to move slowly here.

The second thing I did to pursue my goal of not living out of anyone else's story about work was to pay close attention to the tasks I did every day. For most of my life, I had believed that work has a couple of good parts and then tons of parts that just suck. A friend told me he had been at a conference where an organizational psychologist argued that we cannot hope to enjoy more than 20 percent of our work.

Let's do the math on that. In a forty-hour workweek, this would mean you'd have thirty-two hours of boredom, drudgery, frustration, or just plain nonsense. In there somewhere would be a mere eight hours of something enjoyable. Assuming you work forty-nine full-time weeks a year, that is 1,568 hours of work that drains you.

But here's the kicker: Why is that eight hours enjoyable? It is still *work*, after all. It's enjoyable because it is in alignment with your passion, skill set, *and* the fact that God made you a lowercase-c creator.

This last point is really important. If God is our Creator, and we are made in His image, then it stands to reason that we are all called to create. Or as Tim Keller so eloquently put it, work is "rearranging the raw material of God's creation in such a way that it helps the world in general, and people in particular, thrive and flourish."[3]

I need to point out here that the group of "people flourishing" is supposed to include you. Some Christian subcultures think of work only as something that helps *others* flourish (i.e., not ourselves or our own families). I understand this push to get people to not think of *just* their own needs, but when this thinking goes too far, you get a sense that Christians are called only to be martyrs so that others may thrive.

This is another form of scarcity thinking. It says that if only one of us gets to thrive, it should be you. But when Jesus says, "You shall love your neighbor as yourself" (Mark 12:31), He is not arguing that you should love yourself badly, is He? Rather, He is saying you should love yourself and your family well and then turn that love on your neighbors too. Don't diminish that love at all—simply expand it!

So how did I pay attention to the tasks I did every day? I started a journal that I called the Daily Notice.[†] Each night after the kids went to bed, I carved out ten minutes. I got still, let my body and breathing settle, and then got out a blank sheet of paper. I started with a simple bullet list of the activities of the day. These were simple sentences like:

- Met with Byron—had coffee
- Worked on proposal for foundation
- Met with Shana—talked about hiring plan

Each time I wrote a new item, I sat in remembrance of what that moment had felt like. Had I been energized or tanked after the meeting with Jim? I'd write a "+" if I came away from the meeting with a skip in my step, a "0" if I simply felt neutral afterward, and a "–" if I left the meeting feeling exhausted. So it would be:

---

†   I am deeply grateful for the work of the Conscious Leadership Group and their book *The 15 Commitments of Conscious Leadership*. The Daily Notice was influenced by their "Daily Energy Audit."

- Met with Byron—had coffee +
- Worked on proposal for foundation 0
- Met with Shana—talked about hiring plan +

One of the key ideas behind the Daily Notice is something I think of as the "Holy Spirit Breadcrumb Trail to Joy at Work." (Worst title ever, I know. Bear with me as the marketing department makes it catchier.) The idea is simple: when we do work that is in alignment with who God made us to be, we are energized. It's like a little signal from the Spirit saying, "This is what you were made for!" It's a breadcrumb in the sense that it is an indicator of the path we are meant to walk. As if God were saying, "Do more of this, My beloved!"

This idea was made famous in the 1981 movie *Chariots of Fire*. It tells the story of two runners who were getting ready for the 1924 Olympics. One of the runners, a Christian named Eric Lidell, has this beautiful line. Speaking about God, he says, "When I run, I feel His pleasure."[4]

At the end of this chapter, I present the Daily Notice as a practice. Here, I'll say that its goal is to intentionally draw your awareness to the rhythms of your work. Do you feel connected, energized, and ready to go? Or consistently neutral, flat, unaffected? Or drained in such a way that when you come home all you can think about is Netflix and bed? The reality for most of us is that it's a complicated blend of all three every day. The Daily Notice begins to sort through the noise of your days and offers the chance to discover patterns.

Think of this in the context of two meetings. In the first you connect with the people, share ideas that somehow become even better ideas, move a project forward, and come away feeling like you want to pump your fist in the air. I like to think of this feeling as the energy a US women's soccer player gets after scoring a goal. It is all huge smiles while sliding twenty yards across the pitch on your knees. (Seriously, how do they slide so far?) Conversely, the draining I am describing here is that feeling you have after a meeting that you didn't need to have, that had no clear outcomes or point, that felt like everyone was talking over each other, and where no one brought snacks. The worst.

The final step of the Daily Notice is to ask two questions.

The first big question is to look at the things that deplete you and ask, "What can I delete, delegate, or do differently?"

What to do about things you find you can delete is obvious: just stop doing that thing you don't like if you no longer *have* to do it. Sometimes, we are doing things at work that no one asked us to do or that haven't been relevant in years. In my work at Corner to Corner, I was still signed up to attend a bunch of meetings where I was no longer needed. The staff was crushing it and didn't need me to be there. I found that not having anything to add made these meetings particularly exhausting. I checked with the team, and they resoundingly said, "We got this." I happily deleted these meetings from my schedule.

Delegate is also fairly obvious: If you can, give the work to someone else. But here we often run into another false story that goes something like this: "If I hate this kind of task and find it draining, then it is draining for everyone in the world." This is not true. There is a whole class of people called accountants who love spreadsheets. Love them!

At Corner to Corner, I recognized that I was also spending lots of time trying to be a part-time grant writer and grant reporter. This is not at all my sweet spot. With this new awareness from the Daily Notice, we began to seek out someone who could come on staff and do these tasks full-time. When they joined the team, not only did they take over the work with joy (it was aligned with who God had made them to be), it also led to Corner to Corner being awarded several new grants ... because the work was better!

Perhaps the third step, *do differently*, is the most challenging. It can be hard to learn how to change our approach. For all of us, there will be tasks at work that we cannot stop doing or hand off to someone else. This is a wisdom and discernment issue.

For example, I have met very few people who *love* spending lots of time in their email inbox. It is a draining and nonstop task that for most seems like something they can never get ahead of. But if we have to do it, perhaps we can change the way we engage with it.

As I sought to find joy even in my email, I made several changes. First, I no longer did email first thing in the morning. Instead, I gave that time to creative and thought-based work. Second, I created an "email playlist" on iTunes with songs that make me smile and have an infectious backbeat. Third, I timeboxed email so I worked on it for twenty minutes midmorning and twenty minutes midafternoon. These changes had the desired effect of injecting joy into my email work while enabling me to stay on top of communication.

And you know who noticed the change in my communication patterns? No one. It turned out that no one was watching their clock waiting for me to reply within nine minutes of receiving their message. Who knew?

The second big question is to look at the things that give you joy and ask, "Is there a way to do more of this kind of work?"

Initially, you might think, *I don't even know why I love this type of work so much.* If this is the case, get curious. Write it out. Pray it out. Ask the Lord for guidance. Talk to a close friend or colleague whom you respect and get their take.

My Daily Notice showed that I got a ton of joy from connecting with high-energy, curious people who wanted to partner with our work at Corner to Corner. Instead of just letting this be a random occurrence that happened every so often, I started to seek out these kinds of people and partnerships. I found that we were able to grow faster and with more resources when I leaned into this kind of joyful connection. If you move toward the kind of work that gives you that boost of energy and joy, you are following the trail of breadcrumbs toward alignment and purpose!

I know that some might hear these ideas and go, "No, we work only in the world of thorns and thistles. Haven't you read about the fall of man from Genesis?" They will look at the language of Genesis 3 and see all the reasons why they will simply accept that work has to be *primarily* hard. As if to believe that work could be joyful is some sort of pipe dream for the spiritually immature. Or even worse, as if to experience joy in your work would be dishonoring to God. I have seen this play out. Some Christian brothers and sisters I know don't think they are actually doing God's will at work unless it is terrible to endure.

To these dear brothers and sisters, I offer this thought: What if the work of Jesus in bringing about the redemption of all things also includes our work? What if the impact of the cross, the empty tomb, and the tongues of flame of the Spirit was so tremendous that even our work is being changed? Would you dare to believe that God's grace is so extensive that we are called to a completely new view of work? One that is more informed by Luke 24 than Genesis 3? One that is shaped by the empty tomb more than thorns and thistles? How big is redemption? How far does reconciliation go?

John Mark Comer is on to something powerful when he writes, "Everything matters to God. The way of Jesus should permeate and influence and shape every facet of your life."[5] This includes our work, dear friend!

PRACTICE: The Daily Notice—Thirty Days

1. Get still. Let your body and breath settle.
2. Get a blank sheet of paper or your favorite notebook. I keep one just for the Daily Notice.
3. At the top of the page, write the date.
4. Write out all the main things you did at work today. Don't overthink it or get too granular.
5. Slowly go over the list, one item at a time, taking a simple pause at each one. Remember how you felt, what the experience was like. Then just put a "+" to signify that it was life-giving, a "0" if it felt neutral or flat, and a "–" if it drained you.
6. Review the Daily Notice once a week to look for any patterns. When you see lots of "+" marks, get

curious about how you can amplify this activity in your life. When you see consistent "–" marks, ask yourself what steps you could take to delete, delegate, or do differently. Do this for thirty days and then decide if you want to continue.

––––––––––

Epilogue

We Don't Know

I am years into my daily practice, years into cultivating equanimity in the midst of challenges that used to knock me down and keep me down, and yet there are still days when I wake up awash with fear. The lie is that somehow equanimity means we are no longer human. But humans feel all the things. We were made that way. And today, this human still feels fear.

In the past, I would run from fear. Suppress it, ignore it, even shame my fear. The internal emotional experience of this was low-grade dread of self. Have you ever felt something that you didn't want to feel but didn't know how to stop feeling? It is as if one part of you is feeling that thing you don't want to feel and another part of you is screaming, "Stop feeling that!"

I woke up in that state on the morning I wrote this. Nothing had happened. There was no unsettling event the night before. I woke up after nearly eight hours of sleep—two in REM, according to my running watch!—and still I was swimming in fear. It's that kind of nagging anxiety I think many of us have just decided is normal in the hope that if we give it this label it will fade to the background where it can possibly be ignored.

But I am committed to living a different life. A life where my fear is known, embraced, understood, and released. So this morning, in the dark before the house stirs, I make a cup of coffee in my bedroom (K-Cup, of course), throw on my favorite comfy joggers, and relax into the chair I have placed "just so" next to the window.

As I sit, the fear swirls around, rising and falling. I breathe. I get still. And I move toward curiosity. Internally, this is very uncomfortable. At age forty-five, I have decades of practice avoiding, minimizing, and suppressing fear. So moving toward the fear is like walking in ever-thickening mud.

There is resistance.

But I move closer still. I greet my fear. I say simply, "Good morning. I see you." I ask my fear what shape it takes this morning.

It doesn't quite reply so much as "float" answers, like throwing a tennis ball in zero gravity. It teaches me something: I am afraid of losing a key colleague at work. That I depend on them so much, and to lose them would be devastating. Okay, good. That's part of it. Is there more?

I stay with the curiosity. I go deeper in my questioning that is simultaneously embracing and accepting. My fear tells me that underneath this fear is the fear of failure. The fear of being seen to take a huge risk and falling on my face. This is the fear of shame. Of humiliation. It is that particular fear that remembers when I gave an excited answer to a teacher in third grade, sure that I was right, only to hear her say, "Not even close." The other children laughed at me for trying so hard. Why do I still try so hard? I stay with the fear. I breathe.

I feel my body settle into the chair. I feel my bare feet on the cold, wooden floor. I sip my coffee, thankful for the caffeine. I stay with the fear. Some part of me asks, "Will I always be afraid?" *Sometimes.* I say this with no shame or blame. I say this with gentle acceptance. My fear feels this and relaxes further. I invite the Spirit to come and be fully present. The Spirit kindly reminds me that He is always right here with me.

I am awash in love. My innermost self feels the joy and presence of the God who made me in love and made me for love. In that moment, in the perfect loving stillness, I feel my fears fully release. I ask my fears what the future holds. They reply in a delighted half laugh, *We don't know!*

I whoop with delight. I almost wake up Tiff. "We don't know" is right! My fears do not know the future. *Because that is what my fear most wants*: to know and control the future. But here, now, breathing steadily, gently, patiently, awash in the love promised and delivered from ages past, my fear knows that it is okay to not know. Someone else does know. And that someone can be trusted. God's got us.

I open my eyes. I breathe. I smile. I hear Raylan yell for me as he wakes up. I step into the day.

A Note about the Practices

Skills of a very high order can be
maintained only with daily practice.

Charlie Munger, "The Psychology of Human Misjudgment"

It is important for me to remind you that I am not a psychologist, a neuroscientist, or a PhD in anything. I am a practitioner.

Everything you have read in this book comes from a deeply personal place, a place where I was like a drowning man grasping onto anything that might get him one more breath. The drowning man has no time for theory. There is a terrifying clarity that comes when one is looking into the abyss: something either works or it does not work. What you find in this book are the practices that worked for me.

I do not offer you a theory. I offer you a practice. I cannot say this strongly enough: ideas are useless unless you put them to work.

It reminds me of a house that was being built in my neighborhood. The builder dropped off all the supplies: tons of wood, stacks of drywall, and even a large, plastic-wrapped square full of insulation. The plan seemed very clear, and it looked like construction would start soon.

But then a few days went by, and no one was at the job site. A few weeks later, still no activity. Over the next few months, the careful piles of materials started to break down, exposed to the elements. Ultimately, all the supplies began to rot, decay, or bleach out in the sun. They were rendered useless.

If you approach the practices of Spirit-led self-awareness with intention but no action, they will have exactly zero impact on your life.

Now, I do not mean this to sound like some cruel motivational speech given by your gym trainer. I do not think we can do activities for long if we do them from white-knuckle discipline. We can start some kinds of personal growth this way, but the cost is a crusty, dried-out soul. I do not recommend it.

My invitation to you would be to do the work, but do the work with play. Do the work with an awareness of what you can and cannot take on every day. Do not try to force these practices, but gently step into them. Find the first practice that resonates with your soul, and start there.

If I had to recommend one place to start, it would be on the practice I've called the emotional trailhead. The emotional trailhead is still the first thing I do every single day, and it has planted the seeds for the fruit of the Spirit over and over again in my life.

But beyond that first recommendation, you will find no designated order here. This is not a system with a simple five-step formula. You must "try on" the practices, see which ones fit and which ones do not. Explore. Play. Connect with the Spirit as you connect with yourself. May you find the practice that fosters the most joy in your life.

There are no elevators to Everest, but there are guides. May you find this book to be a useful guide on your journey.

Acknowledgments

Let me thank some incredible people who made this possible:

Tiffany, my first reader—without your support this would not have happened.

Raylan and Penelope—thanks for letting me lock myself in the room to write.

Mom and Dad—thanks for being willing to grow and change with me. I love you.

Chris, Tony, and Austin—y'all are incredible. I can't wait to see what happens next!

Jon, Bennett, and Molly—thank you for encouraging me each step of the way.

Matt—decades of friendship is such a gift!

Bryan—I'm so grateful for your friendship and wisdom.

Jim—the morning walks shaped my thinking for this book.

Wes—thanks for pointing me further into the mystery.

Shana and the Corner to Corner team—y'all have been steadfast prayer partners on this journey!

John Blase and the team at Bindery—thank you for seeing the potential in this project!

And finally, to the fantastic team at David C Cook—your support, advice, and collaboration has been so much fun.

There are so many other people who I could thank here who poured into me in big and small ways. You know who you are. Thank you.

Notes

Introduction

1. John Calvin wrote, "Our wisdom, in so far as it ought to be deemed true and solid Wisdom, consists almost entirely of two parts: the knowledge of God and of ourselves" (Institutes of the Christian Religion, chapter 1, quoted in "Knowledge of God and Self," Ligonier, accessed November 20, 2024, www.ligonier.org/learn/articles/knowledge-of-god-and-self?srsltid=AfmBOooV_7p7xa3hHvED V97j3ayF-gdLbNkHTFaqRcxxo88mRA8-Cvo0). Take for example Thomas Aquinas's thoughts on the opacity of self and the need to intentionally learn the self: "Learning about a thing's nature requires a long process of gathering evidence and drawing conclusions, and even then we may never fully understand it." Therese Scarpelli Cory, "Thomas Aquinas—Toward a Deeper Sense of Self," *Fifteen Eighty Four* (blog), Cambridge University Press, January 24, 2014, www.cambridgeblog .org/2014/01/thomas-aquinas-toward-a-deeper-sense-of-self.

2. St. Augustine, *The Confessions*, ed. Maria Boulding (Hyde Park, NY: New City Press, 1997) 5, 7.

Chapter 1: The Spirit in You

1. See "Enneagram Type 8: The Challenger," Enneagram Institute, accessed August 29, 2024, www.enneagraminstitute.com/type-8.

2. Martin Luther King Jr., "Loving Your Enemies," sermon, Dexter Avenue Baptist Church, Montgomery, Alabama, November 17, 1957.

3. Hugo D. Critchley et al., "Slow Breathing and Hypoxic Challenge: Cardiorespiratory Consequences and Their Central Neural Substrates," *PLOS ONE*, May 14, 2015, https://doi.org/10.1371/journal.pone.0127082; Xinjun Yu et al., "Activation of the Anterior Prefrontal Cortex and Serotonergic System Is Associated

with Improvements in Mood and EEG Changes Induced by Zen Meditation Practice in Novices," *International Journal of Psychophysiology* 80, no. 2 (May 2011): 103–11, https://doi.org/10.1016/j.ijpsycho.2011.02.004; "In general, slow breathing techniques enhance interactions between autonomic, cerebral and psychological flexibility, linking parasympathetic and CNS activities related to both emotional control and well-being." Andrea Zaccaro et al., "How Breath-Control Can Change Your Life: A Systematic Review on Psycho-Physiological Correlates of Slow Breathing," *Frontiers in Human Neuroscience* 12 (September 2018): 353, https://doi.org/10.3389/fnhum.2018.00353.

Chapter 2: To Breathe

1. Anthony De Mello, *Awareness: Conversations with the Masters* (New York: Image Books, 1990), 36.

Chapter 3: Shift Work

1. George I. Viamontes and Charles B. Nemeroff, "Brain-Body Interactions: The Physiological Impact of Mental Processes—The Neurobiology of the Stress Response," *Psychiatrry Annals* 39, no. 12 (2009): 975–88.

2. Dario Maestripieri and Christy L. Hoffman, "Chronic Stress, Allostatic Load, and Aging in Nonhuman Primates," *Development and Psychopathology* 23, no. 4 (2011): 1187–95, https://doi.org/10.1017/S0954579411000551.

3. Thomas Merton, *Choosing to Love the World* (Louisville, CO: Sounds True, 2008), 27.

4. Andrea Zaccaro et al., "How Breath-Control Can Change Your Life: A Systematic Review on Psycho-Physiological Correlates of Slow Breathing," *Frontiers in Human Neuroscience* 12 (September 2018): 353, https://doi.org/10.3389/fnhum.2018.00353; Gary G. Berntson et al., "Heart Rate Variability: Origins, Methods, and Interpretive Caveats," *Psychophysiology* 34, no. 6 (November 1997): 623–48, https://doi.org/10.1111/j.1469-8986.1997.tb02140.x; Masaki Fumoto et al., "Appearance of High-Frequency Alpha Band with Disappearance of Low-Frequency Alpha Band in EEG Is Produced during Voluntary Abdominal Breathing in an Eyes-Closed Condition," *Neuroscience Research* 50, no. 3 (November 2004): 307–17, https://doi.org/10.1016/j.neures.2004.08.005.

5. Danielle Rousseau, "Neuroplasticity—Rewiring Your Brain through Mindfulness," Boston University, December 5, 2023, https://sites.bu.edu/daniellerousseau/2023/12/05/neuroplasticity-rewiring-your-brain-through-mindfulness.

Chapter 5: All the Drama

1. "Badwater Ultramarathon," Wikipedia, accessed August 29, 2024, https://en
.wikipedia.org/wiki/Badwater_Ultramarathon.

2. For information on the human brain's "default mode networks" that influence
this kind of behavior, check out: Michele W. Berger, "What Happens in the Brain
When We Imagine the Future?," Penn Today, May 17, 2021, https://penntoday
.upenn.edu/news/Penn-neuroscience-research-what-happens-in-brain-future
-imagining.

3. See Viktor Frankl, *Man's Search for Meaning*; Craig Groeschel, *Winning the War
in Your Mind: Change Your Thinking, Change Your Life*; David Goggins, *Can't
Hurt Me: Master Your Mind and Defy the Odds*—but be forewarned his language is
salty and it is NOT written for kids—and the letters of Marcus Aurelius, to name a
few. Now, a critical note on victim mindset: Please don't confuse this with actually
being a victim. Abuse, oppression, and heinous acts are committed against our
vulnerable neighbors. They are actual victims, and we dare not treat them as if they
have not been victimized.

4. Stephen B. Karpman, "Fairy Tales and Script Drama Analysis," *Transactional
Analysis Bulletin* 7, no. 26: 39–43, https://karpmandramatriangle.com/dt_article
_only.html.

5. The best and most useful articulation of the drama triangle that I've found is
from the book *15 Commitments of Conscious Leadership* by Jim Dethmer, Diana
Chapman, and Kaley Warner Klemp. I can't recommend it enough.

6. "Neuroplasticity," *Psychology Today*, accessed August 29, 2024, www
.psychologytoday.com/us/basics/neuroplasticity; Joyce Shaffer, "Neuroplasticity
and Clinical Practice: Building Brain Power for Health," *Frontiers in Psychology*
7 (July 2016): 118, https://doi.org/10.3389/fpsyg.2016.01118; Caroline White,
"Brain Circuitry Model for Mental Illness Will Transform Management, NIH
Mental Health Director Says," *BMJ* (September 2011): 343, https://doi.org
/10.1136/bmj.d5581; Richard J. Davidson and Antoine Lutz, "Buddha's Brain:
Neuroplasticity and Meditation," *IEEE Signal Processing Magazine* 25, no. 1
(December 2008): 174–76, https://doi.org/10.1109/MSP.2008.4431873; Robert
M. Sapolsky, *Why Zebras Don't Get Ulcers* (New York: Henry Holt, 2004).

Chapter 6: Problems to Solve

1. *Merriam-Webster*, s.v. "accretive," accessed August 29, 2024, www.merriam-webster
.com/dictionary/accretive.

2. Martin Buber, *I and Thou*, trans. Walter Kaufmann (New York: Scribner, 1970).

3. Anina Rich and Sarah Maguire, "What Is the Baader-Meinhof Phenomenon?," Lighthouse, July 22, 2020, https://lighthouse.mq.edu.au/article/july-2020/What -is-the-Baader-Meinhof-Phenomenon.

4. Learn a lot here: Dhanalakshmi Harikrishnan, "Reticular Activating System: Definition and Function," November 21, 2023, https://study.com/academy/lesson /reticular-activating-system-definition-function.html. Or see a more technical paper here: Richard Leblanc, "The White Paper: Wilder Penfield, the Stream of Consciousness, and the Physiology of Mind," *Journal of the History of the Neurosciences* 28, no. 4 (October–December 2019): 416–36, https://doi.org/10.108 0/0964704X.2019.1651135.

Chapter 7: The Gift of Consistency

1. "Amygdala," Cleveland Clinic, accessed August 29, 2024, https:// my.clevelandclinic.org/health/body/24894-amygdala.

2. "The History of Cognitive Behavior Therapy," Beck Institute, accessed August 29, 2024, https://cares.beckinstitute.org/about-cbt/history-of-cbt; Stefan G. Hofmann et al., "The Efficacy of Cognitive Behavioral Therapy: A Review of Meta-Anaylses," *Cognitive Therapy and Research* 36, no. 5 (July 31, 2012): 427–40, https://doi.org/10.1007/s10608-012-9476-1.

3. Robert Boyd Munger, *What Jesus Says* (Grand Rapids, MI: Fleming H. Revell, 1982).

Chapter 8: Emotions—WTH?

1. "Nates Christian Parents," Nate Bargatze—Topic, YouTube, accessed August 29, 2024, www.youtube.com/watch?v=F6s2_qnsfcs.

2. "Epictetus," Wikipedia, accessed August 29, 2024, https://en.wikipedia.org/wiki /Epictetus.

3. Bill Bright, "Experiencing the Adventure," Cru, accessed August 22, 2024, www .cru.org/us/en/train-and-grow/transferable-concepts/walk-in-the-spirit.html.

4. Goran Šimić et al., "Understanding Emotions: Origins and Roles of the Amygdala," *Biomolecules* 11, no. 6 (May 31, 2021): 823, https://doi.org/10.3390 /biom11060823.

5. John Bradshaw, *Healing the Shame That Binds You*, Recovery Classics Edition (Deerfield Beach, FL: Health Communications, 2005), 144.

6. Curt Thompson, *The Soul of Shame: Retelling the Stories We Believe about Ourselves* (Downer's Grove, IL: InterVarsity Press, 2015), 9.

7. Peter Scazzero, *Emotionally Healthy Spirituality: It's Impossible to Be Spiritually Mature While Remaining Emotionally Immature* (Grand Rapids, MI: Zondervan, 2006), 5.

8. Jim Dethmer, Diana Chapman, Kaley Warner Klemp, *The 15 Commitments of Conscious Leadership: A New Paradigm for Sustainable Success* (Conscious Leadership Group, 2015).

9. Chip Dodd, *The Voice of the Heart: A Call to Full Living* (Nashville, TN: Sage Hill, 2015).

10. Robert Plutchik, "The Nature of Emotions," *American Scientist* 89 no. 4 (July–August 2001): 344–50, www.jstor.org/stable/27857503.

Chapter 9: Alignment

1. C. S. Lewis, "The Weight of Glory," sermon, Church of St. Mary the Virgin, Oxford, England, June 8, 1941, published in *Theology*, November 1941, and by the SPCK, 1942.

2. Anthony De Mello, *Awareness: Conversations with the Masters* (New York: Image Books, 1990), 61.

3. For more on this, see Anthony De Mello's book *The Way to Love*.

Chapter 10: Scarcity

1. Alexandria White, "77% of Americans Are Anxious about Their Financial Situation—Here's How to Take Control," CNBC, updated September 25, 2024, www.cnbc.com/select/how-to-take-control-of-your-finances.

2. Lynne Twist, *The Soul of Money: Transforming Your Relationship with Money and Life* (New York: Norton, 2006), 120.

Chapter 11: Flow

1. Estimation based off the solopreneur number of $26,084 in revenue, https://advocacy.sba.gov/wp-content/uploads/2020/06/2020-Small-Business-Economic-Profile-US.pdf.

2. "One Third of Your Life Is Spent at Work," Gettysburg College, accessed August 29, 2024, www.gettysburg.edu/news/stories?id=79db7b34-630c-4f49-ad32-4ab9ea48e72b.

3. Timothy Keller, *Every Good Endeavor: Connecting Your Work to God's Work* (New York: Dutton, 2012), 47.

4. "God Made Me Fast," *Chariots of Fire*, directed by Hugh Hudson (1981; Burbank, CA: Warner Home Video, 2010), DVD.

5. John Mark Comer, *Garden City: Work, Rest, and the Art of Being Human* (Grand Rapids, MI: Zondervan, 2015), 109.

DAVID C COOK

JOIN US.
SPREAD THE GOSPEL.
CHANGE THE WORLD.

We believe in equipping the local church with Christ-centered resources that empower believers, even in the most challenging places on earth.

We trust that God is *always* at work, in the power of Jesus and the presence of the Holy Spirit, inviting people into relationship with Him.

We are committed to spreading the gospel throughout the world—across villages, cities, and nations. We trust that the Word of God will transform lives and communities by bringing light to the darkness.

As a global ministry with a 150-year legacy, David C Cook is dedicated to this mission. Each time you purchase a resource or donate, you're supporting a ministry—helping spread the gospel, disciple believers, and raise up leaders in some of the world's most underserved regions.

Your support fuels this mission.
Your partnership sends the gospel where it's needed most.

Discover more. Be the difference.
Visit DavidCCook.org/Donate